Consulting with Parents and Teachers

by

JOSEPH H. BROWN
*Associate Professor of Educational Psychology
and Counseling, University of Louisville*

and

CAROLYN BROWN
*Counselor-Consultant, Southern Indiana Mental Health Center,
Jeffersonville, Indiana*

CARROLL PRESS
Publishers

43 Squantum St., Cranston, R. I. 02920

About the Authors —

   JOSEPH H. BROWN is an Associate Professor of Educational Psychology and Counseling at the University of Louisville. He received a Ph.D. in counseling from Indiana University. After working in the University of Kentucky Teacher Corps, he accepted a position at Louisville where his major interests have focused on parent training, family counseling, and parent/teacher consultation. He currently serves as a District Advisor with the Behavior Analysis Follow Through Program University of Kansas, where he consults with teachers and other school personnel.

   CAROLYN BROWN received her Ed.D. in counseling from Indiana University. She is currently on the staff of the Southern Indiana Mental Health Center where professional duties involve conducting workshops and counseling adults and children. She consults with parents and teachers in surrounding school districts.

Library of Congress Cataloging in Publication Data

Brown, Joseph H.
   Consulting with parents and teachers.

   Bibliography: p.
   Includes index.
   1. Parent-teacher conferences. 2. Child development. 3. Behavior modification.
   I. Brown, Carolyn S. II. Title.
LC225.5.B76   371.1'03   81-10100
      ISBN 0-910328-35-8 (cloth); ISBN 0-910328-36-6 (paperback)
                                                          AACR2

Manufactured in the United States of America

CONTENTS

ILLUSTRATIONS: Figures and Tables

PREFACE

Two important points provided the motivation for our writing this book. The first is the belief that consultation has not been practically presented as a systematic behavioral process of implementation and evaluation. Consequently, we present the "how-to" of consultation. We begin with the request for consultation and bring the reader, in a step-by-step manner, through the process of consultation.

Secondly, the number of counselors available in the schools is not commensurate with the need for counseling services. Consulting is perhaps the most viable alternative to counseling both in terms of time and efficiency. There is little question concerning the expediency of consultation over the provision of direct services because working directly with children is obviously a more time-consuming process than is the dissemination of information and suggestions. Furthermore, by acquainting teachers and parents with techniques for modifying children's behavior, the number of students who will ultimately be reached is multiplied. Teachers and parents typically generalize from one situation in which they receive consulting help to other situations. If a technique, approach or strategy is helpful with one client, a consultee will likely try similar but perhaps modified approaches with other children whose behavior is inappropriate.

This book is intended to be a practical guide for persons in the helping professions, particularly for school counselors, school psychologists, and social workers. For the most part, consultation has been defined differently by different people, but unfortunately it has not been described in a way that enables the counselor trainee to learn the skills necessary to consult. We have conceived of consulting as a process in which the client's behavior is changed through direct intervention of the consultee or through change in the consultee's behavior which ultimately results in changed client behavior. Our purpose in writing this book is to define a systematic model of consulting which can be applied to individual clients. Inherent in the model is an evaluation process which allows the consultant to continually monitor progress toward preestablished goals. Consequently, evaluation of the process depends on the degree of change in client problem behavior.

Chapter One describes the general model, and additional chapters focus on various subsystems of the model. Following the first chapter each chapter contains a post-test of information covered and a task analysis and instructions for implementing various sub-skills within the larger skills. The trainee's performance can be evaluated at a cognitive level, then, but more importantly can be evaluated by his/her ability to implement these skills with consultees.

Clearly, this book can serve only as a guide to consultation. The person who utilizes consultation techniques is obligated to use his/her own sensitive, creative, and flexible ideas in implementing strategies specifically tailored to the needs and abilities of the individual consultee. Our chief purpose and hope is that the readers will feel more comfortable and more competent in assuming the role of consultant as a result of reading this book.

Joseph H. Brown
Carolyn Brown

Louisville, Kentucky
August, 1981

1

THE CONSULTING MODEL

A major challenge confronting the helping professions is that of providing the necessary services to those who need them. The population from which counselors, social workers, psychologists, and other mental health personnel are drawn is already being drained to its maximum capacity. Furthermore, the rapid growth of the population in this country and the continuing changes in society will likely increase the variety and frequency of behavioral problems. And, the public is not entirely convinced that these helping professions can offer viable solutions for the vast array of behavioral problems. There is ample data to indicate the widespread use of drugs, the apathy of students at all levels of the educational process, and the large numbers of unemployed graduates of high schools and universities, and the obvious question is: What are the helping professions doing to alleviate these problems?

The increased concern about the effectiveness of the helping professions is reflected in administrative decisions regarding staffing. All too often when budgets are cut, these services are reduced and consequently, the number of people directly receiving treatment is reduced. In 1970, the Joint Commission on Mental Health of Children estimated that one and one-half million children under the age of eighteen were in need of immediate professional assistance and at that time only thirty percent were receiving assistance. One must conclude, then, that in the future, perhaps more than in the present, the shortage of persons in the helping professions will necessitate that behavioral problems be dealt with by those other than "professional helpers" who relate directly to the client in the natural environment.

Thus, the focus must shift from training persons who give direct services to training persons who function as consultants. The consultant may be a counselor, school psychologist, social worker or possibly a learning disabilities specialist. While in most cases it is clear who the consultant is, this may not be quite as clear in other

1

instances. Generally, the person providing help to the change agent is labeled the consultant (Bergan, 1977). That is, the consultant is one who works with another person (consultee) to help a third party or parties (Dustin and Burden, 1972). While this book focuses on teachers and parents as consultees, administrators, case workers and others who work with children may also fall into this category. In some cases the child may be the consultee. For example, a child may be helped in dealing with his/her alcoholic father. Although the consultee receives the attention of the consultant, it is the third party (client) who is the focus of intervention (Dustin & George, 1973). For example, when a parent contacts a case worker for help with his/her child, the parent is the consultee and the child is the client. Consulting is the direct communication between the consultant and the consultee. It is the consultee who is helped in dealing directly with his/her clients. The process of helping the client by direct communication is often called therapy or counseling. (See Figure 1.)

The help provided to the teacher or parent may be either preventive or remedial. Psychological education programs (DUSO, Magic Circle, etc.) are examples of preventive projects and can be taught to large groups of students, with the goal of improving interpersonal skills. Likewise, specific learning activities can help to reduce cognitive or perceptual deficits. The hallmark of these programs is that they can be easily integrated into the regular school curriculum. By providing mental health education at an early age, many problems can be alleviated before they become so severe they warrant remediation.

Because of the wide range of consulting functions, it is difficult to determine effectiveness, and it is particularly difficult to specify the conditions, times, persons, and problems with which consulting can be effective. This is because the definitions are often vaguely defined and fail to provide specifications for what the consultant will be doing on the job. Unless a systematic analysis of the consulting process is made, there can be no standards by which counselors or psychologists can compare their own practices.

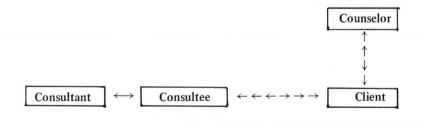

Figure 1: **Diagram of the Consultant and Counseling Process**

Consultant Role

The primary role of the consultant is (a) to assist the consultee (e.g., parents, teachers) in specifying the desired terminal behaviors for the client and the factors contributing to the problem, and (b) to facilitate the consultee's acquisition and implementation of the mutually agreed upon procedures (Mayer, 1973). This may require special knowledge of how to handle a problem and can be facilitated by providing parents or teachers with written material on dealing with their children. Once the teacher or parent has selected appropriate techniques from these readings, the consultant might assist them in implementing them. Regardless, the effectiveness of the consultant is ultimately based upon his/her ability to facilitate the consultee in reaching his/her objectives with the client.

The process of reaching these objectives requires the consultant to move the consultee through each step of the consulting process. (See Figure 1.) It is crucial that the consultant describe this process to the consultee and explain how s/he will operate. Through appropriate verbal behavior, the consultant may guide the consultee through each step of the process to reach the mutually agreed upon objectives. In addition the consultant provides a set of specialized knowledge and techniques to alleviate the problem and reach the objective.

Consultee Role

The role of the consultee is first to provide a description of the problem s/he is having with the child. Once the problem has been discussed and goals and plans to reach those goals established, the consultee must decide whether s/he will implement the suggested plan. Likewise, the consultee must decide which things (i.e., observing the child, gathering achievement data) s/he is willing to do to carry out the program. In this respect s/he has a great deal of control over how and when the consultation program is carried out.

Client Role

The role of the client is to change his/her behavior in the desired direction. For example, if the child needs to improve on getting along with others, hopefully s/he will be able to do that as a result of the consultation program. Provided that the child is old enough, s/he should help in establishing goals or agree to the amount of work to be completed by a certain date. By allowing the client to participate in the program, s/he will more likely be committed to it.

Consulting Process

The consulting process can be best described through a model which sequences the various activities involved. This requires systematically operationalizing each step of the consulting process and facilitates the consultant's assessment of effectiveness with the consultee. Each component of the consulting process is listed in Figure 2.

Prior to consultation, the consultant is obligated to help the consultee (i.e., parent and teacher) determine when the consultant's services are needed. When someone runs a fever for several days, s/he calls a doctor. S/he knows that the doctor has the skills to bring the fever down. Likewise, a teacher and parent must be able to recognize certain behaviors and know how to deal with them. That is, if parents and teachers can agree on a normal rate of social and academic progress, then each will know when to request the consultant's services.

The consultant in this case can often be of help initially by assisting the school and community in defining the critical minimum objectives required for language, arithmetic, or social interaction skills. Once critical instructional and social objectives are paired with a time criterion, parents and teachers can project a minimum rate for a child to reach the critical objectives.

Teachers can obtain regular, periodic measures of each child's progress toward meeting the critical objectives. Such a system helps the teacher and parent determine when to request help from the consultant. However, while critical minimum objectives can offer the consultee an optimum way to determine when to request outside help, this is often not the case. Rather, the consultee must often assist parents and teachers in determining when to seek outside help in the absence of stated objectives. Here, the consultant may describe his/her services to faculties, PTAs and civic clubs. In each case, the consultant should describe situations in which the teacher and parent should seek help outside the classroom.

While consulting guidelines will differ, a teacher or parent can be fairly certain that consultation is needed (1) if the child's social behavior continues to interfere with academic work, (2) if the child continually interferes with other students' academic or social behavior, (3) if the child interferes with the teacher's ability to operate effectively, or (4) if the child is unusually withdrawn (O'Leary & O'Leary, 1972). Unless the teacher or parent is able to handle these problems, a request for consultation should be made.

Receive Request for Consultation

The request for consultation may be made through personal contact, by telephone, or indirectly. After receiving the referral the

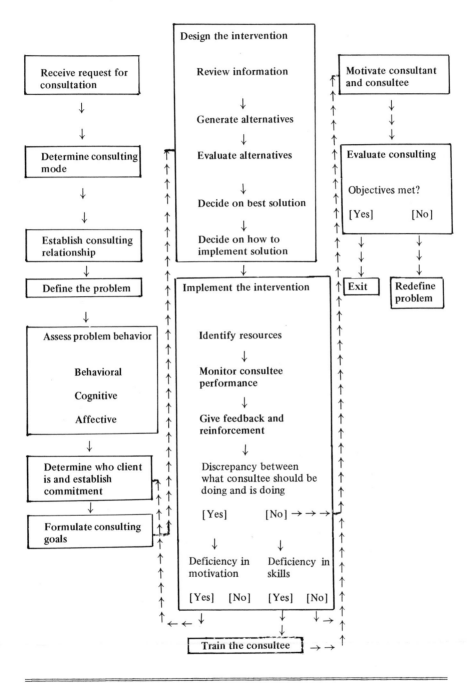

Figure 2: **The Consulting Model**

consultant should avoid removing pupils from the situation or providing a quick solution because in so doing s/he is assuming a counselor role (taking responsibility for the child). Rather, the consultant should schedule an appointment with the parent or teacher to discuss the problem. Here, there is a better opportunity to review the situation under more relaxed conditions.

Regardless of how the meeting is arranged, the consultant will want answers to a specific set of questions about the nature of the problem and how the consultee has dealt with it. If there is direct communication, the consultant may ask for supplementary information, not only about the client's behavior but about the consultee's environment. The consultant will want to know the situational context in which the client's behavior occurs, i.e., conditions under which undesirable behavior occurs and does not occur, the norms of that setting, the frequency of the undesirable behavior, and the level of desirable behavior.

If the consultant decides to become involved, an initial contract or agreement should be established with the consultee. This should be a preliminary contract which stipulates (a) consultant's and consultee's roles, (b) date treatment begins, (c) amount of time required, (d) resources, and (e) persons responsible for implementation. Such a preliminary contract often points out discrepancies in the amount of time each party wishes to commit to the program, so anticipated benefits and costs should also be a part of this initial agreement. In many cases, the costs to the consultee, consultant and child can be minimized. Unless this occurs, the program will have little likelihood of success.

The consultant is not always in a position to collect information about the client. In this case, the consultant can request that the consultee provide additional client information and may, thereby elicit the further cooperation of the consultee. Rather than perceiving these as unnecessary intrusions, the consultee will often interpret this as a sign that the consultant is interested in the consultee's dilemma.

Determine Consulting Mode and Role

The first step of a consultation program focuses on the consultant who must first establish his/her role and be mindful of the services s/he is able to provide. In defining the role, the consultant must be aware of his/her skills and should make public at the outset those services s/he is able to provide. After the problem is defined and goals are formulated, the consultant must decide what mode of consultation will be used. The consultant may prefer the prescriptive mode in which s/he prescribes a solution for the consultee, s/he may wish to coordinate efforts of several consultees in changing a client's behavior, or s/he may wish to problem-solve or use the collaboration mode of consultation. Regardless of the mode or combination of modes, however, s/he should be specific about how s/he will work with consultees.

Establish Consulting Relationship

The consultant's success or failure in a given situation is at least partly dependent upon his/her ability to form a non-threatening, yet helpful atmosphere for the consultee. By the very nature of the consulting process, the basic power relationship between the consultant and consultee is that of peers. That is, the consultee is continually free to participate or not participate in the consulting process and is also free to accept or reject it. At the time of the initial request for help, the classroom teacher or parent may not know how to manage the child's behavior or even how to interpret the many behaviors which ordinarily would be classified as problematic or deviant. Feelings of inadequacy may, therefore, arise when an "expert" comes into the house or classroom to assist with these problems. The consultant should avoid confrontation and instead help the consultee become more relaxed by promoting a positive relationship. Good listening behaviors such as eye contact and verbal following reinforce the consultee's speaking and thus encourage further discussion. If the consultee feels comfortable and expects to be helped by the consultant, s/he is more likely to stay involved in the process and to accept some of the ideas generated.

In developing a relationship, the consultant must always be mindful of the effect his/her verbal relationship is having on the parent or teacher. In the initial stages of the interview, the consultant is exploring the nature of the problem with the consultee. The consultant may ask the consultee to provide background and environmental information (e.g., medical information or parent-child relationships) about the client. In addition, the consultant should help the client explore the problem by responding and summarizing consultee responses and asking open-ended questions. These responses help the consultee to feel understood and facilitate the process toward problem identification.

When the consultant is unsure of what the consultee is saying, s/he may clarify by asking the consultee what s/he means by a certain statement. Clarification responses also help consultant and consultee reach agreement or disagreement with regards to problem-related factors (Bergan & Tombari, 1975). Clarification is often required to insure agreement on the client problem conditions under which the problem occurs. Likewise, clarification is necessary in goal setting and in designing and implementing the plan for change.

Define the Problem

At this stage, the consultant assists the consultee to discuss specific problems s/he is having with the client and to note discrepancies between the child's existing behavior and desired behavior. For example, if the child completes only half his/her assignments and you wish him/her to complete all of the assignments, then the problem area is quite explicit. In an interview, using appropriate questions and reinforcers, the consultant leads the parent or teacher to describe the child's behavior and identify specific problems. Moore & Sanner (1969) note that during the consulting relationship, the consultant's responses can reinforce the teacher's descriptive statement of behavior. On the other hand, when the parent or teacher responds with vague (nonperformance) terms such as "aggression" or "hostility" or "poor attitude," the consultant should determine what is meant by these generalities. For instance, how is a "good attitude" manifested? Does it mean that the child will smile more? Does it mean that s/he will comply with parental requests? Unless the problem behavior is specified in observable terms, the effectiveness of the consultant's intervention cannot be measured.

Often, the consultant will think of several problem behaviors manifested by the child. Here s/he should attempt to explore all the related problem areas and then give priority to the problem area that is of greatest concern to the consultee. This can often be determined by deciding which problem is of greatest immediate concern and which problem is easiest to monitor. For instance, stealing may be a critical behavior but is very difficult to monitor. In contrast, social interaction skills and academic behaviors are easy to monitor and may lead to a reduction in more severe behaviors such as stealing (Graziano, 1971).

Once the problem area has been specified, the consultant and consultee must determine those factors contributing to the problem (i.e., environmental conditions which affect client behavior). These can be determined by the consultant asking the parent or teacher what happens before or after the problem behavior.

Once the problem area has been specified, any constraints which mitigate against its resolution must be identified. For example, a husband may be displeased with his wife when she begins to give attention to their child. A teacher may be discouraged from implementing a new program with his/her pupils because it will not meet with the approval of the principal. Unless the consultant discusses these potential barriers and the ways to reduce them, the consultee may likely resist implementation.

Assess Problem Behavior

After learning to specify problem behaviors and to acquaint the consultee with role and function, the next step is to begin assessing problem behaviors in the behavioral, cognitive and affective areas (as appropriate). Systematic observation, tailored to events of particular interest, is a valuable and versatile technique which can be employed in the home and classroom.

In some instances, however, observing behavior in the natural environment presents special problems. For example, a teacher may find it extremely difficult to monitor "on-task" behavior during a reading lesson, but this problem may not exist during a "silent reading period." Therefore, it is advisable to select a setting that presents the fewest problems. As the observer becomes more competent in recording data, the observations may be shifted to more complex settings.

The consultant must also consider that behavior may change simply because of the presence of the observer. It is important, then, that either the teacher who is always present makes the observations or that the students become desensitized to an outsider who comes in to observe.

Once the consultant has made sure clients have become adapted to the observer and has identified a setting where the behavior may be observed, s/he must establish a level at which the behavior typically occurs. The record of this level is usually referred to as a baseline. Knowledge of the base rate of the client's behavior strengthens the consulting process in three ways. First, it permits the consultant and consultee to tailor the intervention to the client's needs. Secondly, it may tell the consultee and client where to begin the intervention. For example, if a child is only completing fifty percent of his/her assignments, the teacher may at first set a goal for completing sixty percent of the assignments. Thirdly, the base rate helps the consultant to evaluate the effectiveness of the consulting processs. That is, if the client's behavior changes in the desired direction from the base rate, the intervention can be considered effective.

In addition to gathering base rate data, initial observations of the client in the problem situation provides clues as to what is maintaining the problem. By using a log or diary, teachers and parents can record what occurs before and after the problem behavior. Likewise, similar controlling events can be recorded before and after positive behavior.

The preceding procedures can be used by the consultant to verify the problematic behaviors reported by the consultee. Also, the observations by a second party will be helpful in determining if this is a common classroom behavior or if it is specific to one child. Once the consultant has made observations, the consultee (parent or teacher) can clarify with him/her which behaviors are referred to by labels such as "hostile," "aggressive" or "rude." If there is a discrepancy between what the parent or teacher reports and what is observed, it may be necessary for the consultant to probe the parent or teacher for more information. At this point, the consultant must determine a reason for the discrepancy and decide who owns the problem.

It is crucial here for the consultant not to assume responsibility for the problem. Often a parent or teacher will want the consultant to do something about the child's problem. The consultant must make it clear that s/he will assist the teacher or parent in efforts to resolve the problem but that s/he will not do it for them. Whenever this issue arises, it might be important to provide a list of services that the consultant "can" and "cannot" provide.

Once the problem has been verified, those factors which are maintaining the client's undesirable behavior must be identified. Feedback from these observations can serve as a basis for designing a behavior change program, i.e., observational data may show behavior patterns such as the reinforcers which are maintaining undesirable behavior. For example, a teacher's criticism may be maintaining a child's aggressive behavior.

Identification of reinforcers which maintain behavior is particularly difficult when responses are being maintained on very thin reinforcement schedules. That is, the reinforcer may be presented so seldom that it fails to be noticed by the observer. Or, the consultee may fail to report what she or he is doing when the child is behaving inappropriately. A teacher or parent might say "I was just standing there." Here, the consultant can encourage the consultee to record on a log form what he or she was doing prior to and following the problem behavior. Preliminary descriptions of the child and a seating chart demonstrating his/her placement should also be used.

In order to obtain this information, the consultant might provide the consultee with a set of procedures for observing the client. Observations should be systematic, and the behavior to be observed should be discrete enough to make systematic observation possible. By concentrating on one client at a specific time, the consultee is able to reduce the complexity of the problem and analyze the situation for relevant information. For example, the child may be talking to another child during a particular instructional activity. Examination might reveal that s/he had completed his/her work and that the talking occurs only when the work is completed. The consultee (teacher) might observe others to see if talking occurs at the end of the lesson. If it does, the consultant and consultee might consider some strategies to encourage the child to move on to the next lesson.

Once the problematic behavior and controlling factors have been verified, the consultant and consultee must determine whether the nature of the client's problem warrants a referral to a specialist. Stewart et al. (1978) specify that a client should be referred when (a) time and facilities are not available to treat the problem, (b) the counselor-consultant lacks the necessary skills to treat the problem, and (c) consultees (e.g., teachers, parents, classmates, siblings) cannot be identified to treat the problem.

When a referral is made, the consultant should explain to the consultee that while another individual or agency will be providing assistance with this particular concern, s/he can return to see the consultant if s/he needs help with other problems. Any resistance to termination such as the consultee's dependency upon the consultant should be discussed.

Determine Who the Client Is

The answer to the critical question, "Who is the client?" determines whether a relationship is primarily for consulting or therapeutic purposes. If the consultee is in a position to change undesirable behaviors, then a consulting relationship exists. Conversely, if the consultee is not in a position to change the undesirable behavior, another consultee (peer, principal, parent or teacher) should be identified. Obviously, the problem as well as ownership of the problem must first be specified. For instance, if the teacher makes numerous demands on Jimmy or reports that she becomes "irritated when she's with him," the problem may well be the teacher's, depending upon whether this problem generalizes to other situations. The goal then is to change the teacher so that the client's behavior may subsequently be changed.

Formulate Consulting Goals

While it is important for consultees to describe maladaptive behavior in performance terms, it is also essential that alternative behaviors exhibited by the child be described operationally. These alternative behaviors should be positive alternatives to the negative behaviors that are to be extinguished. For example, rather than fighting the teacher or parent may wish the child to be studying or interacting positively with peers. When teachers or parents are uncertain about what they consider to be desirable, it may be helpful for them to identify a few "well-behaved" students and observe their behavior.

Although there is usually general agreement about the selection of desirable behaviors, complete accord is not always reached. Who has the right to specify a desirable behavior for an individual? — the child? the teacher? the consultant? When consultees (parent or teacher) disagree, further discussion between the concerned parties must be reached before a program is instituted. As a general rule, consent from parents and other legal guardians is necessary before the intervention program is implemented. For maximum program effectiveness, agreement on target behaviors by potential consultees is imperative.

Once alternative desirable behaviors have been specified, the consultant and consultee should discuss the probable consequences for each behavior. The consultant often must prompt the consultee, "What would likely happen if Jack were to be more accepted by his peers?" "Is this behavior likely to be supported by others?" Once the desired behavior has been selected, objectives should be specified in order to reach the goal (e.g., interacting more with peers). Each objective should specify the behavior (asking questions), the conditions in which the goal behavior is to occur (playing Monopoly) and the criterion level for each goal (five questions per hour).

By stating goals in positive behavioral terms, the consultant and consultee have avoided the labels which might suggest pathology or disease. Furthermore, the focus is on observable behaviors which can be agreed upon and treated, thereby avoiding misunderstanding and confusion over whether or not the goals are reached.

Design the Intervention

The aim at this stage of the consulting process is designing a specific plan which the consultee will implement to achieve desired goals. Here the procedures developed for the problem and goal definition are interfaced with a program implementation plan (Parker, 1975). When the consultee has defined the problem and goal behavior, s/he is ready to develop a procedure and will state how the goal and objectives will be reached. Deciding on how to remedy the undesirable situation is a problem-solving process between the consultant, consultee and any interested parties. Problem-solving is a process which (1) provides a variety of potentially effective responses to the problem situation and (2) increases the probability of selecting the most effective responses from among the various alternatives (Goldfried & Davison, 1976). The underlying assumption is that the consultee may have some ideas on how to change his/her behavior and will be more committed to it if s/he has some input into how that change should take place.

In this stage the consultant offers recommendations in the form of suggestions (e.g., "You might want to try . . .") or prompts (e.g., "What could we do about . . ."). These suggestions and prompts allow the consultee to provide solutions to the client problem or accept or reject the consultant's recommended suggestions. Once the plan has been discussed, it is important to ask the consultee to summarize it. This helps to insure that the consultee understands and accepts the plan of intervention.

Once the recommended procedure has been identified, a written intervention plan should be drawn up. While the sequence and nature of the functions of the plan will differ because of selected goals and other factors, the intervention plan should include the following:

1. Client objectives

2. Reinforcers for the client's desirable behavior; for the consultant's and consultee's desirable behavior

3. Procedures for decreasing undesirable behavior

4. Procedures for increasing desirable behavior

5. Individuals who will reinforce the client's desirable behavior

6. Resources the consultee will need

7. Individuals and methods to prompt the client and consultee

8. Individuals who will collect data

9. Individuals to provide training, if needed, for the consultee

10. Dates to begin and end program

11. Individuals to be notified of the program

This outline should be presented to the consultee and any reluctance or disagreements with the recommended procedures should be discussed. Often a parent or teacher will say s/he wants to help a child, but in actuality, s/he is angry with the child and resists helping him/her. Unless this resistance is acknowledged and the consultee's role is specified, the program should not be implemented. The consultant can often elicit a commitment from the consultee through a verbal agreement or a written contract.

Implement the Intervention

The implementation of the consultant's recommendations is a critical matter for the consultee. Since the consultee is assuming responsibility for the client, it is important that the consultee be able to implement the intervention within his/her role position. For example, if a teacher is asked to implement a program which is inconsistent with his/her teaching responsibilities, the program will likely fail or be discontinued once the consulting relationship has been terminated.

The consultant often finds it necessary to reinforce the consultee's use of appropriate behavior. This immediate and frequent reinforcement is necessary until the progress of the client begins to reinforce the consultee's behavior. For example, once it has become apparent to the teacher that the behavioral change program is effectively modifying pupil behavior, the consultant can reduce the amount of praise directed toward the consultee. Typically, the consultee (teacher or parent) should design and be responsible for executing the program, while the consultant should provide support and offer assistance.

Periodic meetings of the consultant and consultee to discuss the success of the program are helpful. At these meetings the consultant should check with the consultee to determine if there is agreement between the program design and the program currently being implemented. Any unforeseen problems which arise should be resolved. In addition, new functions should be added if necessary. Finally, the consultant and consultee should assess the progress the child is making toward his/her objective.

Decide Whether or Not Training for the Consultee Is Needed

Many consultees will require assistance from the consultant in finding out how to go about implementing his/her recommendations. This is often an essential part of the consultant's contribution and is another reason why s/he should discuss the written recommendations with the consultee.

There are a number of ways the consultant can determine whether the consultee needs additional training. First, the consultant might ask the consultee to role-play to determine whether the consultee has the necessary skills to modify the client's behavior. The consultant might also observe the consultee during treatment to insure that treatment is being properly implemented. If the consultee needs additional skills, the consultant might provide written materials and/or video tapes which model the desired behavior. Or, the consultant might demonstrate the necessary skills to the consultee and then ask the consultee to rehearse them until they are mastered.

Motivate the Consultant and Consultee

A critical question here is, "Who will provide reinforcement to the consultee, client and consultant?" This is an important question because the ill fate of many projects may be partly attributable to the changing reinforcers experienced by the staff. Initially, such positive reinforcers as prestige might be predominant while later in the program, boredom with routine or failure of clients to improve often becomes prominent. The consultant in this instance can specify goals for him/herself and the consultee. Furthermore, the consultant should identify colleagues who might be supportive of his/her efforts in order that reinforcement is maintained.

Evaluate Consultation

Evaluation should be based upon the mutually agreed upon objectives of the consultant and consultee. The criteria for each objective should determine the success/failure of the consultation. If the level of client performance during implementation of the plan corresponds to the level of performance specified in the objectives, consultation may be terminated. Criterion level of performance may often be determined by an increase in performance from pre-intervention (baseline) and the intervention period.

In other cases, multiple baseline across behaviors, clients, or conditions is one of the most common ways to demonstrate a functional relationship between the intervention and the client's behavior. Multiple baseline refers to measuring more than one target behavior for a particular client or measuring changes on a specific problem for multiple clients or situations. Once a relationship has been established, the consultant and consultee should consider follow-up maintenance and generalization procedures since behavior which has been modified will persist and generalize only if the environment is supportive of the altered behavior.

If goals have not been reached, the consultant and consultee should discuss the problem again so that a new plan can be implemented. Here, the consultant should request feedback from the consultee about his/her behavior and describe what s/he did or did not do that led to the observed outcomes during consultation. Each activity should be described in terms of success or failure and why this result occurred. Even when objectives have been reached, the consultee may react negatively to the client's behavior. In these instances the consultant and consultee may need to increase the criterion level of performance or select new goals.

In summary, there have been numerous attempts to seek more effective consulting procedures since it is so widely recommended as a legitimate professional responsibility (Whitley & Sulzer, 1970). Indeed, many counselors, school psychologists and social workers want to reach more students through effective consultation. However, while the consulting role has been frequently discussed in the literature, there have been few attempts to design systematic procedures.

2

BEGINNING CONSULTATION

A good consultation program starts with good organization. That is, the consultant must define his/her role (beliefs and practices) for helping consultees (parents, teachers) solve their problems. Successful role definition is often based upon two major factors. First, the consultant must be aware of his/her skills — his/her training and success in resolving problems. This information should be incorporated into the role definition. Secondly, s/he must determine the type of consultation that s/he wishes to use.

Types of Consultation

Caplan (1970) identifies four major types of mental health consultation. These are (a) client-centered case consultation, (b) consultee-centered case consultation, (c) program-centered administrative consultation, and (d) consultee-centered administrative consultation. Each of these will be described in turn.

In client-centered case consultation, the consultee asks for help in dealing with a particular client or group of clients. Essentially, the thrust is to help the consultee understand the nature of the client and the client's problems and thereby increase the consultee's capacity to work more effectively with problem children in the future.

In consultee-centered case consultation, primary attention shifts from an understanding of the client to those aspects of the consultee's own behavior which may be detrimental to working with a client or group of clients. For example, a teacher may unknowingly be rewarding disruptive student behaviors by attending to them consistently. Caplan identifies four types of consultee-centered case consultations, based on (1) lack of knowledge, (2) lack of skill, (3) lack of self-confidence, and (4) lack of professional objectivity. The example given here would be of the first type, lack of knowledge.

In program-centered administrative consultation, the focus is on either how to develop a new program or how to improve the existing one. Here, the consultant comes into the organization, studies it, and makes recommendations about how the organization can be changed. In this type of consultation, it is assumed that the organization does not have the resources to solve its problems so the resources of an "expert" are solicited. An example of this type of consultation would be an outsider coming in and helping to set up a new program for the gifted, learning disabled, etc.

The fourth type of consultation, and according to some experts, the most difficult, is consultee-centered administrative consultation. Here, it is assumed that the organization has the resources to solve its problems but for some reason it is not using these resources effectively. An example where such consultation is warranted would be a school where goals are not being met due to poor staff morale, ineffective leadership from the principal, staff resistance to authority, and poor communication across the staff.

Consultation Modes

In addition to these four types of consultation, Caplan also identifies three *modes* of consultation: the prescription mode, the mediation mode and the collaboration mode. These are described separately.

Prescription Mode:

In the prescription mode of consulting, the consultant is requested to observe and assess a child's behavior and prescribe how the problem can be solved. The prescription mode is often used by outside consultants in residential centers or mental health clinics. In some cases, however, the consultant may be a psychologist who resides within the school system but is located outside a specific school. In both situations, the prescription mode involves the consultant giving clear directions about what should be done to solve the client's problem. That is, if a child is having learning problems, the consultant identifies these and prescribes a remedial program. Since this approach depends on a body of knowledge and skills of the "expert" consultant, the consultee must "buy" into the plan or the consultant has little to offer.

There are several other problems with this mode of consultation. First, while teachers or parents may accept the plan, they may not implement it properly (Kurpius & Brubaker, 1976). Or, in some cases, by accepting the recommendation of the consultant, the consultee becomes less involved and fails to question whether the procedure is likely to work in the context it is to be administered (homeroom, kitchen, etc.).

It is critical, then, that if the consultant wishes to use a prescription mode of consultation s/he develop evaluation measures on a daily basis. This may be difficult if the consultant (e.g., mental health worker) works outside the institution where s/he consults. In this case, someone should be responsible for monitoring the program and reporting the results each day. If the consultant wishes to use a prescription mode of consulting s/he might describe the role as: "I will arrange a time to test and observe him. Then in approximately two weeks I will send you a report containing recommendations," or "Johnny's problem seems to be . . . . . These are my recommendations for helping him."

Mediation Mode:

When the consultant is using the mediation mode, s/he is likely working with the parent, teacher and others (social worker, principal, etc.) in the child's environment. Mediators are people who (1) possess reinforcers valued by the child, and (2) can dispense them when called on. This is an appropriate mode where each role group (teacher, social worker, parent) is working independently with the child. Here the consultant will coordinate the functions of each role group member.

In the mediation mode of consultation, the consultant will organize initial meetings, collect data from the mediators and assist the mediators in identifying the problem and objectives (Carrington, 1976). Unlike the prescription mode, the consultant negotiates with the mediators (consultees) about what procedures will be applied and what sources of influence utilized. In addition, the consultant discusses and agrees on an implementation and evaluation procedure. Just as in the prescription mode, the consultant and consultee continually monitor the program to insure its success in producing client change. If the consultant wishes to use a mediation mode of consultation, s/he might describe the role as: "You seem to be having a problem with Joe. I would like you to make some initial observations. Once you have done this, we will meet with the principal and Joe's parents and decide how to resolve this problem. I will be available and responsible for coordinating the program."

Collaboration Mode:

In this mode, rather than *prescribing* or *coordinating*, the consultant *assists* the consultee in defining, developing and implementing the program. The collaboration mode is largely predicated on the problem-solving process. Consultees are reinforced for defining the problems and generating solutions. Hence, the consultee takes more ownership in the consultation program. The consultee is more likely to select a procedure that fits his/her particular situation, and a more trusting relationship is likely to exist since the consultant and consultee are mutual partners in the consultation program. Finally, program changes are more likely to be maintained since the consultee has taken more ownership in the program. A common role statement for the collaboration mode of consultation would likely be: "Together we can define the problem and consider some alternative solutions."

Exercise: **Consultation Modes**

Directions: Given the following role statements, indicate whether each statement is indicative of (p) prescription, (m) mediation, or (c) collaboration modes of consultation.

. . . . . . 1.   I will assess the child's abilities and give you some written recommendations to carry out.

. . . . . . 2.   Together we can consider some alternative solutions to the problem.

. . . . . . 3.   We can decide how much influence you have with the child.

. . . . . . 4.   I will coordinate the program and help you find a solution for the problem.

. . . . . . 5.   I will assist you in defining the problem and developing a solution.

Answers: 1. (p); 2. (c); 3. (m); 4. (m); 5. (c)

The skills the consultant should possess might be different depending upon the mode of consultation selected. For example, if the consultant selected a prescription mode of consultation, s/he would likely need a great range of diagnostic and intervention skills. While these skills are important in the mediation and collaboration modes, problem-solving is most important in the collaboration mode. Coordination and knowledge of social influencing are critical to the mediation mode of consultation.

The consultant is not obligated to use one specific mode. Rather, s/he can use skills from several modes. The crucial factor, however, is that the consultant specify the role to the consultee. Because many consultants are reliant on the consultee to implement and maintain the program. The remainder of this book will focus primarily on skills within the mediation and collaboration modes of consultation.

The primary consulting approach described in this book is client-centered, case-oriented, using the collaboration mode. Some attention is given to consultee-oriented case consultation, however, particularly in the areas of skill deficits and knowledge. In fact, Chapter Eight is devoted to training the consultee.

It should also be noted that while the focus is case-oriented, these cases will reflect varying degrees of severity. Many problems brought to the consultant are full-blown and demand immediate attention. Others will reflect students who are risks for future problems, e.g., students who have poor interpersonal skills. Still other problems may be predictable ones as a result of development or transition, e.g., from home to kindergarten, and intervention will be designed to prevent problems from occurring. The consultant may be working at varying levels of prevention, then. The example of the crisis situation represents tertiary prevention, the work with students who are risks represents secondary prevention, and the "anticipatory guidance" represents primary prevention.

Each consultant operates from a variety of assumptions, skills and values. Obviously, it is impossible to define all of these values and assumptions clearly, but there are some reasons for the consultant to make known his/her personal philosophy or frame of reference. First, by making these ideas public, it insures that the consultant is aware of his/her biases and how they affect his/her work at school. Secondly, if parents or school personnel know the consultant's position, it will considerably reduce the likelihood of a consultant/consultee impasse or time-consuming disagreements regarding procedures (Parker, 1975).

Whether a consultant works on the "inside" (school) or "outside" (mental health center), s/he should make assumptions, values, etc. known to his/her public. This can often be done through brochures, handouts, or a presentation to a faculty or PTA. For example, if the consultant feels that a child's behavior is determined by environment, the approach to consultation will include a variety of techniques for altering the environment. By including these beliefs in a brochure and explaining how s/he has altered problems in the past, the consultant helps the public to better understand how they might ask for help.

Request for Consultation

Inside Consultation

Consultants who reside within a school are often contacted informally in the lunchroom or hallway. Regardless of how the contact is made, however, the consultant's first response is the beginning of the consulting relationship. For example, a consultant may be contacted in the hallway by a teacher, "Jeff is driving me crazy. Can you talk to him?" Given this situation, the consultant should indicate a willingness to see Jeff in order to understand his perceptions of the problem but should also set a convenient time for meeting with the teacher to define the problem specifically. If the teacher says s/he is "too busy" or that the "consultant should just work with Jeff," this may be done initially. Then, in conveying information to the teacher, it will likely be possible to further define the problem area and discuss what may be maintaining it in the classroom.

Behavior checklists may be another initial approach to get the teacher involved. If, however, after defining the problem, the teacher shows no interest in dealing with Jeff's problem behavior, the consultant must determine what the likely outcome of working with Jeff would be and this depends on the problem area. If Jeff is experiencing non-school related problems, perhaps working with him or with him and his parents would be helpful. On the other hand, if the problem is school-related and the teacher shows no interest in getting involved, the consultant may delay working with the child until the parent or teacher becomes willing to take part in the change program.

If the consultant attempts to work with a child who is referred by the teacher or parent when they are maintaining the problem, s/he is generally setting him/herself up for defeat because any change in the child effected by individual counseling may be counteracted by the teacher or parent. Secondly, if the program fails, it only reinforces what the teacher or parent may have already expected (e.g., that the child cannot be helped). It should be noted, however, that in cases where the child/parent or child/teacher relationship is poor, the consultant may teach the client skills for changing the teacher's or parent's behavior. Thus the consultant should avoid closing a case abruptly. This can also cause the teacher or parent to lose confidence in the consultant and continue to treat the client (child) in the same manner as before.

If a teacher or parent shows resistance when the initial referral is made, it is usually effective to wait until the problem becomes of sufficient magnitude to warrant parent/teacher involvement. Often the willingness of a consultee to enter into a personal contract with the consultant depends in part on whether there is a crisis situation. If the consultee is really searching for help, s/he is more likely to assume ownership of the problem and not try to make it the responsibility of the consultant. If the consultee does try to have the consultant assume responsibility for a case, it may be handled as follows:

Consultee: I can't do anything with him. I just don't have time. I think it would help if he could just talk with you.

Consultant: Well, I think we identified some things that might improve Mike's behavior. I don't think I could do anything for him unless these things were changed.

Consultee: Well, I don't know what I can do about it.

Consultant: I'm sure you are as concerned as I am. Do you think we need to set up another meeting to talk about this?

Consultee: OK.

In this dialogue, the consultant failed to take responsibility for the problem but maintained a good relationship with the consultee.

It is critical that the consultant not provide a "quick solution." This may be detrimental, first because it is unclear what the problem is and the teacher or parent may just want to "complain," and secondly, quick solutions are often rejected by the consultee. A quick solution suggests that the problem really may not be serious and deprives the teacher or parent of the opportunity to complain. If the teacher or parent feels that s/he is not being understood, s/he will not likely discuss the problem with the consultant again. However, if the consultant listens to the teacher or parent and schedules an appointment to discuss the problem further, they will be better able to clarify and define the problem under relaxed conditions. There are times when a discrepancy exists between the client's, consultee's, and consultant's perceptions of the problem and until these are clarified, it is quite possible that no client change will occur (Kurpius & Brubaker, 1976).

Outside Consultation

Unless the consultant is providing a regular service to a school or residential center, contact for an outside consultant (mental health or social worker) will likely be by phone or letter. Since the consultant in this case will usually have little information regarding the problem, the consultant should be cautious about assuming any responsibility until s/he has observed the child or set up a meeting with the referral source (parent, teacher, principal, etc.). After adequate information is obtained, the consultant is in a better position to determine which course of action should be taken and to assess how concerned the teacher or parent are and how likely they are to follow through.

Establish Time for Next Meeting

Before the consultant meets with the teacher or parent again, s/he should gather additional information related to the problem. If time permits, visiting the class to observe the child may be helpful. If not, the consultant might give the teacher or parent a pre-interview checklist to complete. (See Tables 1, 2, 3.)

The pre-interview checklists can serve two important functions: (1) to develop a language system that will allow the consultee to communicate with the consultant, and (2) to provide an ecological assessment of the child's behavior. The consultee's conception of human behavior may be radically different from that of the consultant, making it more difficult for useful information to be produced (Wahler & Cormier, 1970). Pre-interview checklists not only help the consultant and consultee to adopt a uniform language but also help the consultee look more specifically at the problem areas. In many cases, the consultee describes problem behaviors in general terms which do not give the consultant adequate information. The completion of the pre-interview checklists can further this information and make the initial interview more productive.

Explain Consulting Relationship

During the initial interview, the consultant should try to understand the problem and how the consultee perceives it. Inherent in this understanding is some discussion of the extent to which the problem behavior is affecting the consultee as well as the consultee's expectations of how the child should act. In such a discussion, it is possible to determine whether or not the consultee has unrealistic expectations and then clarify these. The following dialogue provides an illustration of this.

Teacher: He is a very defiant child. I wish you would talk to him.

Consultant: Sounds like he really bothers you. What does he do?

Teacher: When I tell him to do something, he does just the opposite.

Consultant: I've got an appointment right now, but could we get together after school and talk some more about this?

Teacher: OK.

Consultant: Maybe I can work with you to figure out what we can do to change his behavior.

Teacher: What do you mean?

Consultant: Well, we can discuss what seems to be the problem and try to set a goal for changing his behavior. Then we will try to identify some procedures you might use to reach the goals. We can measure our success by the change in his behavior.

Notice the consultant's frequent use of "we." This helps to establish a collaborative relationship where the consultee (teacher) feels support. If the consultee feels that s/he is not being understood or if s/he wonders what the consultant will be doing, the consultant might say, "We can decide on what resources and time we have for resolving the problem." It is unwise at this point, however, to be too specific unless the consultant is merely saying, "I will be responsible to you for reaching the goals for the client as long as those goals are agreeable to me."

It is extremely important at this point not to confront the consultee or suggest that s/he is responsible for the client's problem. The consultee generally does not feel s/he is responsible for the client's behavior and in many cases does not think that s/he can control it within the context in which it occurs. This is the time at which the consultant suggests that s/he will be working directly with the consultee on a set of procedures s/he can use with the client. In many cases, resistance will emerge. The consultee may want the consultant to handle the problem situation, may think s/he has already done everything that can be done in the classroom, and may view consultation as a means for the consultant to avoid "responsibility to the child."

Attend to Consultee

Crucial to understanding the consultee's expression of the client's problem is the ability to attend to him/her, both to verbal statements and nonverbal behavior. Obviously, a lack of attention would make the consultee feel the consultant is not interested in him/her and would likely result in resistance or low expectations for help.

Ecological Interview: Out-Patient Child Behavior Therapy*

Table 1: **Child Community Behavior Checklist**

The following checklist allows you to describe your child's problems in various situations outside the home. The situations are listed in the column at the left and common problem behaviors are listed in the row at the top. Examine each situation in the column and decide if one or more of the problem behaviors in the row fits your child. Choose those that fit the best — if any.

	Always has to be told	Doesn't pay attention	Forgets	Dawdles	Refuses	Argues	Complains	Demands	Fights	Selfish	Destroys toys or property	Steals	Lies	Cries	Whines	Hangs on or stays close to adult	Acts silly	Mopes around	Stays alone	Has to keep things in order	Sexual play
In own yard																					
In neighbor's yard or home																					
In stores																					
Public park																					
Downtown in general																					
Church or Sunday school																					
Community swimming pool																					
In family car																					

* Reprinted with permission of author and publisher, from R.G. Wahler and W.H. Cormier, The Ecological Interview: A First Step in Out-Patient Child Behavior Therapy. *Journal of Behavior Therapy and Experimental Psychiatry*, 1970, 1, 279-289.

Table 2: **Child Home Behavior Checklist**

The following checklist allows you to describe your child's problems in various home situations. The situations are listed in the column at the left and common problem behaviors are listed in the row at the top. Examine each situation in the column and decide if one or more of the problem behaviors in the row fits your child. Choose those that fit best — if any.

	Always has to be told	Doesn't pay attention	Forgets	Dawdles	Refuses	Argues	Complains	Demands	Fights	Selfish	Destroys toys or property	Steals	Lies	Cries	Whines	Hangs on or stays close to adult	Acts silly	Mopes around	Stays alone	Has to keep things in order	Sexual play
Morning:																					
Awakening																					
Dressing																					
Breakfast																					
Bathroom																					
Leave for school																					
Play in house																					
Chores																					
Television																					

Table 2: **Child Home Behavior Checklist** – *continued*

	Always has to be told	Doesn't pay attention	Forgets	Dawdles	Refuses	Argues	Complains	Demands	Fights	Selfish	Destroys toys or property	Steals	Lies	Cries	Whines	Hangs on or stays close to adult	Acts silly	Mopes around	Stays alone	Has to keep things in order	Sexual play
Afternoon:																					
Lunch																					
Bathroom																					
Play in house																					
Chores and homework																					
Television																					
When company comes																					

Table 2: **Child Home Behavior Checklist** – continued

	Always has to be told	Doesn't pay attention	Forgets	Dawdles	Refuses	Argues	Complains	Demands	Fights	Selfish	Destroys toys or property	Steals	Lies	Cries	Whines	Hangs on or stays close to adult	Acts silly	Mopes around	Stays alone	Has to keep things in order	Sexual play
Evening:																					
Father comes home																					
Dinner																					
Bathroom																					
Play in house																					
Chores and homework																					
Television																					
Undressing																					
When company comes																					
Bedtime																					

Table 3: **Child School Behavior Checklist**

The following checklist allows you to describe your student's problems in various situations. The situations are listed in the column at the left and common problem behaviors are listed in the row at the top. Examine each situation in the column and decide if one or more of the problem behaviors in the row fits your student. Choose those that fit the best — if any.

	Always has to be told	Doesn't pay attention	Forgets	Dawdles	Refuses	Argues	Complains	Demands	Fights	Selfish	Destroys toys or property	Steals	Lies	Cries	Whines	Hangs on or stays close to adult	Acts silly	Mopes around	Stays alone	Has to keep things in order	Sexual play

Morning:

Teacher explains
lesson

Teacher discusses
with group

Silent work
time

Cooperative work
with other students

Oral reading or
class presentation

Line up for
lunch or recess

Hall

Playground

Lunch

Table 3: **Child School Behavior Checklist** – *continued*

	Always has to be told	Doesn't pay attention	Forgets	Dawdles	Refuses	Argues	Complains	Demands	Fights	Selfish	Destroys toys or property	Steals	Lies	Cries	Whines	Hangs on or stays close to adult	Acts silly	Mopes around	Stays alone	Has to keep things in order	Sexual play
Afternoon:																					
Teacher explains lesson																					
Teacher discusses with group																					
Silent work time																					
Cooperative work with other students																					
Oral reading or class presentation																					
Line up for recess or dismissal																					
Hall																					
Playground																					

Relaxation

Ivey (1970) has demonstrated that attending behavior can be taught and has identified three major components of attending. The first of these is physical relaxation. When the consultant is seated in a comfortable, relaxed position, s/he can more readily talk with the consultee than when s/he is very tense and rigid. In fact, the relaxed consultant tends to speak and gesture in a more natural manner and communicates to the consultee that s/he is ready to help and feels some confidence that s/he can help. In contrast, the tense consultant is less likely to be able to attend because s/he is concerned about his/her own behavior and cannot act in a free and natural manner. When the consultant is ill at ease, this is readily communicated to the client and makes him/her feel some discomfort as well.

Eye Contact

A crucial factor in effective attending behavior is eye contact. A consultant who looks at the wall, or out of the window, and does not focus on the consultee not only communicates to the consultee that s/he is not listening, but that s/he actually has a difficult time listening, even when s/he tries to do so. On the other hand, a fixed gaze is as undesirable as no eye contact at all since it is also likely to make the client uncomfortable. Varied eye contact is preferable. Most of the time the consultant should look at the client as they talk, but periodically glancing away will avoid a fixed gaze.

In short, effective nonverbal attending behavior should include the following:

1. The consultant would initially be sitting at a ninety degree angle. When s/he wants to communicate interest to the consultee, s/he can lean forward at a forty-five degree angle.

2. Hands should be at the side or in the lap in a relaxed position rather than fidgeting with something that will distract the client.

3. Eyes should be focused on the client but not in a fixed gaze.

4. The consultant's body should be facing the client, not turned sideways.

5. Feet should be on the floor, not hanging over a chair.

Verbal Following

A third component in good attending is verbal following of what the consultee says. That is, the consultant stays with the topic and shows by his/her responses that s/he has accurately heard the content of the consultee's message. Obviously, there are times when the consultant will not hear or will misinterpret the consultee's statement, but if this happens consistently, it becomes frustrating to the consultee and communicates that the consultant either does not care enough to attend or that s/he does not have the capacity to attend. In either case, it is unlikely that the consultee will want to continue the relationship under such circumstances.

Verbal following serves four functions. First, it lets the consultee know that the consultant understands what is being said. Second, it allows for further clarification and hence better understanding of the problem area. Third, it insures that the perceptions of the problem are consistent for both consultant and consultee. And finally, it is a way to reduce resistance of the consultee. The following interaction is exemplary of verbal following:

Teacher: I'm wondering if it's worth the effort to try to change him.

Consultant: Maybe there are advantages and disadvantages in leaving things the way they are.

Teacher: I guess I've tried everything. I don't think anything I could do will work.

Consultant: You're not optimistic about changing his behavior.

Teacher: No I'm not. But I'd really like to help him. I don't think he's very satisfied with what he does either.

Exercise: **Verbal Following**

Directions: In the following consultant (C) and parent (P) dialogue, identify those statements which indicate verbal following.

. . . . . .   1. (P): I wish I could just run away and avoid all responsibilty.
           (C): It would be good to just get away and forget all the things you have hanging over you now.

. . . . . .   2. (P): Yeah! Junior really gets to me sometimes.
           (C): What does your husband think about him?

. . . . . .   3. (P): He can't stand the way he acts.
           (C): So, it really bothers him too.

. . . . . .   4. (P): Bothers him — he just left the other night — right in the middle of the meal.
           (C): So he just has to get away from it all.

. . . . . .   5. (P): I guess — he knows if he stays he will hit Junior.
           (C): How old are your other children?

Answers: 1.; 3; 4

Ask Questions

Questioning is important both in helping the consultant get information about the problem as well as in getting the consultee to articulate his/her concerns. In this regard, open-ended questions are more effective. Closed-ended questions can be answered by one word or a short specific answer and consequently curtail communication. In contrast, the open-ended question requires the consultee to give views, opinions, feelings, etc. They consequently elicit more consultee verbalization since they cannot be answered by one or two words. Because the closed-ended question often results in reduced consultee verbalization, it may lead to bombarding or further use of closed-ended questions. For example, the following interaction shows how this happens.

Consultant: Is your child bothering you?

Parent: Yes.

Consultant: Is he disruptive?

Parent: Yes.

Consultant: When?

Parent: Every day.

Consultant: How does this make you feel?

Parent: Awful.

With this kind of questioning, the consultant makes very brief responses and as a consequence, the consultant almost completely directs the interview. That is, the consultant sets up a pattern of closed-ended questions and answers for which s/he will unlikely be able to extricate him/herself. In this case, the consultant is implicitly telling the parent that s/he is the authority and knows what is relevant (Benjamin, 1969); and the parent will likely subject him/herself to this only as long as s/he feels that these questions will lead to a solution. On the other hand, because open-ended questions tend not to restrict the consultee to very narrow answers, they elicit more information. For instance the consultant could have asked, "What does Billy do that bothers you?" and have received most of the information that was received from the five questions above. Examples of closed- and open-ended questions are give below:

Closed: Do you like it when Billy doesn't complete his work?

Open: What does Billy do to bother you?

Closed: How many children do you have?

Open: Tell me about your children.

Closed: Did Tom get mad at you because you hit him?

Open: Why do you think Tom got mad at you?

Closed: You're upset today, aren't you?

Open: What seems to be bothering you?

Exercise: Open-ended and Closed-ended Questions

Directions: In the following teacher (T) and consultant (C) dialogue, indicate whether the questions are (o) open-ended or (c) closed-ended.

. . . . . .   1. (T): I just can't get him to do his work.
              (C): Are you angry with him?

. . . . . .   2. (T): He fights sometimes with other children.
              (C): Tell me a little about the times when this occurs.

. . . . . .   3. (T): I wish he wouldn't patronize me.
              (C): What do you mean by patronize?

. . . . . .   4. (T): I wish she weren't so angry with me.
              (C): Tell me about the times she gets angry.

. . . . . .   5. (T): I'm not going to let her boss me around.
              (C): You don't like that?

Answers: 1. (c); 2. (o); 3. (o); 4. (o); 5. (c)

Clarifying Consultee Statements

Clarification is often useful when the consultant wishes to validate a response. That is, rather than guess at what the consultee is saying, the consultant can ask the consultee to clarify his/her response. This often communicates to the consultee that the consultant is interested. For example:

Parent: She just cries and screams when I am around and when I pick her up it gets worse.

Consultant: Are you saying that she has her temper tantrums when she is near you?

Parent: I love my children but sometimes I just really wish I didn't have them around. They get into fights and — oh, do you know what I mean?

Consultant: You love them but you get angry with them too. Is that right?

In each case the consultant is asking the parent to affirm or validate her previous statement. Clarification helps to establish mutual understanding between the consultant and consultee.

Exercise: **Clarification**

Directions: In the following dialogue between teacher (T) and consultant (C), indicate those responses which are examples of clarification.

. . . . . . 1. (T): Mary cries on the playground — and other times — mainly during recess.
      (C): Did you say that Mary cries only on the playground?

. . . . . . 2. (T): So when you do the observation — uh — we can tell what he is doing.
      (C): Are you saying you want me to do the initial observation?

. . . . . . 3. (T): He won't look at me — only on some occasions.
      (C): When are those occasions?

. . . . . . 4. (T): I'm not sure about his work — he seems to have trouble copying the work.
      (C): When does this happen?

. . . . . . 5. (T): Maybe he is just tired and can't do it.
      (C): Are you saying he is just too tired to do it?

Answers: 1.; 2.; 5.

Write Initial Contract

In addition to verbal skills, the consulting relationship can often be enhanced by an initial contract or agreement. Typically, this agreement will be verbal, but it should specify preliminary requirements which might include (a) initial resources, space, time and help, (b) information needed and how it will be gathered, (c) other people (e.g., consultees) who should be made aware of the program, and (d) possible meeting dates. This type of agreement specifies the commitment for each party in gathering information about the problem. If either the consultant or consultee is unable to commit time and effort in gathering information related to the problem, there is little chance the problem will be resolved.

The consultant might introduce the contract by saying:

Consultant: OK, maybe we can jot down some things we'll need to do to better understand the problem. Since there are several things to be done, maybe we could try and reach some agreement on who will do what. Is that OK?

Teacher: Fine.

Consultant: All right. You mentioned his non-responsiveness in class. I'm wondering if I could come in and observe him more closely. Would this be OK?

Teacher: Yes, anytime.

Consultant: When would be the best time?

Teacher: How long would you want to stay?

Consultant: Maybe forty-five minutes each day.

Teacher: About 10:30 would be the best time then since that is when we get back from the gym.

Consultant: Does he seem non-responsive then?

Teacher: Yes, we have group reading at that time and he won't participate even when I call on him.

Consultant: Are there other times when he is non-responsive?

Teacher: Well, during science he doesn't interact much with others on their projects.

Consultant: Would you be able to observe him then?

Teacher: I could during the first half of the period. During the second half I am usually helping others with their projects.

Consultant: Do you have an aide?

Teacher: Yes.

Consultant: Could he make observations?

Teacher: Yes, if you could show him how.

Interaction such as this should lead to specifications for the initial contract. The initial contract should specify the (a) task, (b) date it is to occur, (c) amount of time required, and (d) the person responsible for carrying it out. A sample initial contract (Figure 3) appears on the next page.

In some cases potential costs for gathering information may outweigh the gains. For example, the teacher may feel that it will take too much time to record the frequency of the child's behavior. This is an anticipated cost to the teacher. In this case, the consultant may wish to minimize the costs in three ways. First, he might make the observations him/herself or s/he might train an aide, if available, to make them. Finally, s/he might suggest an alternative recording procedure for the teacher which would require less time. Unless the anticipated costs of gathering information can be minimized or the anticipated benefits outweigh the costs, there will be little commitment to the procedure.

Figure 3: **Sample Initial Contract**

Target Behavior . . . .

Tasks	Date	Amount of Time	Person Responsible
1. Train aide to time sample	9/15/77	1 hour	Consultant (D. Hughes)
2.			
3.			
4.			
5.			

Anticipated Costs   **Strategy to Minimize Costs**

1. *To teacher/parent:*   Train aide to record behavior
   Time to record behavior

2. *To child:*

3. *To consultant:*

Anticipated Benefits

1. *To teacher/parent:* . . . .
. . . .

2. *To child:* . . . .
. . . .

3. *To consultant:* . . . .
. . . .

DECISION: . . . .
. . . .
. . . .
. . . .

Exercise: **Costs of Gathering Information**

Directions: Given the following anticipated costs, state how the consultant and consultee might minimize them.

Anticipated Costs	**Strategy to Minimize Costs**
1. *To teacher:* Principal may disapprove of recording child's behavior	. . . .
2. *To child:* Child may think he is being singled out for special attention	. . . .
3. *To consultant:* Must make special trip to school to discuss recording procedures with teacher	. . . .

Suggested answers: 1. Involve the principal in the program; 2. Have teacher introduce consultant to the class, or have consultant sit where child will not notice him; 3. Phone the teacher at lunch time to discuss recording procedures.

Unless anticipated costs can be identified and minimized, resistance will likely occur on the part of the consultee or consultant. For example, resistance may occur because the consultee fears disapproval from others. In the above exercise, the teacher who fears what the principal might think will likely be resistant. Likewise the teacher or parent who thinks the consultant will expose their "negative behavior ' will likely be resistant to a change program.

When the consultant identifies this type of resistance, the consultant may indicate that what s/he and the consultee discuss will be held confidential and that it will not be shared with other teachers unless they talk about it and agree to it first.

Questions concerning the consultant's role will come up throughout the consulting relationship and should be answered as they arise. For this reason, it is important for the consultant to write down his/her description of the consulting role so that reference can be made to it throughout the program. This will help alleviate any anxieties the consultee has about the consulting relationship.

Determine Who the Client Is

In the collaborative approach to consulting, the client is the one who receives direct help, and the direct help comes from the consultee (parent or teacher) rather than from the consultant. Consequently if a teacher or parent wants to help in dealing with a particular child, the consultant provides help only as it indirectly benefits the client (child). In some cases, the teacher or parent may wish to discuss personal problems. In this instance, the consultant is staying within his /her role only if these "personal problems" relate to the implementation of the program for the client. Otherwise, the consultant can work directly with the teacher or parent in a counseling capacity. The client is the person with the problem, and behavior change of the client is the primary goal (Tharp, 1975).

It should be noted that in some cases, the consultee may not be able to work effectively with the client because of his/her own problems. For instance, the overweight mother (consultee) may have difficulty avoiding punishment for her overweight daughter (client) when the daughter goes off of her diet. That is, the mother, because of her own feelings (guilt) about her weight, cannot stick to positive reinforcement for "good" behavior, but punishes when "bad" behavior occurs. In such a case, counseling for the mother may result in her being able to conform to the treatment plan suggested for the client.

Another example in which counseling is necessary before consulting can be effective is given below.

Mother: I tried to do what we talked about last time. I responded to John's feelings about being left alone and when he slept in his own bed, I praised him. But my husband said I'm silly to listen to his whining and he threatened to whip John if he got out of his bed. I feel like we're going in opposite directions.

Father: It would help if she didn't yell at me in front of John, especially saying things like, "You're really going to make him afraid of everything."

Consultant: Sounds like you don't agree on how to deal with John and he is aware of your disagreements.

Father: Yes. She's always telling me I do everything wrong and she says so in front of John.

Mother: Only because we come here to learn what to do with John and you never do what we're supposed to.

Father: If you'll recall, I tried talking with John and you came into the room and said, "I think you're just confusing him." I don't think I could do anything to please you.

In this example, consultation about approaches to help John will be futile until the parents are willing to stop criticizing each other and present a united front to John. Consequently, the consultant may first work with them on settling their conflict before going on with a specific intervention for John.

CONSULTING SKILLS INVENTORY

Directions: After each item, check YES or NO to indicate whether the skill has been demonstrated.

BEGINNING CONSULTATION	YES	NO
1. Receive request for consultation	. . . . .	. . . . .
2. Determine consulting mode and role	. . . . .	. . . . .
3. Establish time for next meeting	. . . . .	. . . . .
4. Explain consulting relationship	. . . . .	. . . . .
(a) Attend to consultee	. . . . .	. . . . .
(b) Ask questions	. . . . .	. . . . .
(c) Clarify consultee statements	. . . . .	. . . . .
5. Write initial contract	. . . . .	. . . . .
6. Determine who the client is	. . . . .	. . . . .

* * * * *

CRITERION TEST

Directions: Complete the following statements. Choose (a) (b) (c) or (d).

1. The consultant and consultee can often identify problems and settings in which they occur through
   - (a) projective tests
   - (b) behavior problem checklists
   - (c) scaled questionnaires
   - (d) pre-interview checklists

2. When the teacher contacts the consultant in the school, the consultant should
   - (a) listen and establish a time for further discussion
   - (b) identify the problem
   - (c) establish a goal
   - (d) provide a solution to the problem

3. Which mode of consultation does the following role statement fit? "I will help coordinate our efforts to produce a desired change in the child."
   - (a) provision
   - (b) mediation
   - (c) collaboration
   - (d) prescription

4.   For the following anticipated costs of gathering information related to the problem, give a strategy for minimizing that cost.

To parent: Must observe during lunch time
To child: Must give up play time to be observed

. . . .

. . . .

5.   Which of the following questions is open-ended?

(a)   Do you like him?
(b)   Are you punishing him when he comes home late?
(c)   How many children do you have?
(d)   Tell me more about your class.

6.   Three important elements of attending are:

(a)   eye contact, verbal following, and head nodding
(b)   eye contact, open-ended questions, arms at sides
(c)   eye contact, physical relaxation, and verbal following
(d)   eye contact, verbal following, and perception checking

7.   Clarification is a skill which helps the consultant

(a)   reach a mutual understanding
(b)   open the interview
(c)   determine the appropriate intervention
(d)   close the interview

8.   Given the following parent response indicate a consultant statement of verbal following:

Parent: I don't care what he thinks of me.

(a)   Tell me more about this.
(b)   Why do you say that?
(c)   Whose problem is this?
(d)   Sounds like his opinion doesn't matter to you.

Answers:

1.   (d)
2.   (a)
3.   (b)
4.   Eat lunch early
5.   (d)
6.   (c)
7.   (a)
8.   (d)

3

DEFINING THE PROBLEM

The purpose of defining problems in behavioral terms is to help the consultee describe the client's behavior as s/he views it and to understand the specific behaviors or situations which are causing the consultee some distress. Also, it allows the consultant to determine exact behavioral referents for the labels used by the consultee in describing the problem. Once the problem is translated into behavioral terms, those events which appear to be maintaining or controlling the problem can be determined, then the consultant and consultee can formulate mutually agreeable goals and design and implement an intervention to alleviate the client's problem behavior.

There are several crucial steps the consultant can take in facilitating problem definition. First, s/he can assist the consultee with discussing all of his/her concerns and then put those concerns in their order of importance. When the consultee has decided which problems s/he wishes to focus on, the consultant helps the consultee to define the problems in observable terms and specify those conditions which are maintaining the problem.

Identify All Concerns

For a given class, or even for a given client, the consultee may be able to list several behaviors or conditions which warrant change. In such a case, the consultant should encourage the consultee to name all the problem areas. Obviously, they cannot all be dealt with initially, but it gives the consultant a broader understanding of the client's or class's range of behavior.

Sometimes the consultee has difficulty in describing the problem. However, the consultant can often obtain the necessary information by asking the consultee or others to complete a behavior problem checklist. (See Table 4.)

Table 4: **Behavior Checklist***

				Observable Improvement		
Student's name . . . .

Completed by . . . .
(include title)

Date . . . . .Date . . . .

(Fill in this side at termination.)

Is this a problem?   Observable Improvement

YES	NO			None	Some	Much
. . . .	. . . .	1.	Failure to begin assignments on time	. . . .	. . . .	. . . .
. . . .	. . . .	2.	Incomplete assignments	. . . .	. . . .	. . . .
. . . .	. . . .	3.	Daydreaming	. . . .	. . . .	. . . .
. . . .	. . . .	4.	Walking around the room	. . . .	. . . .	. . . .
. . . .	. . . .	5.	Hitting other children in the classroom	. . . .	. . . .	. . . .
. . . .	. . . .	6.	Hitting other children on the playground	. . . .	. . . .	. . . .
. . . .	. . . .	7.	Make noises for attention	. . . .	. . . .	. . . .
. . . .	. . . .	8.	Does not mix well with other children	. . . .	. . . .	. . . .
. . . .	. . . .	9.	Seems to have no friends	. . . .	. . . .	. . . .
. . . .	. . . .	10.	Steals	. . . .	. . . .	. . . .
. . . .	. . . .	11.	Lies	. . . .	. . . .	. . . .
. . . .	. . . .	12.	Resents authority	. . . .	. . . .	. . . .
. . . .	. . . .	13.	Does not respond to praise	. . . .	. . . .	. . . .
. . . .	. . . .	14.	Unusually shy and withdrawn	. . . .	. . . .	. . . .
. . . .	. . . .	15.	Very negative attitude	. . . .	. . . .	. . . .
. . . .	. . . .	16.	Other:	. . . .	. . . .	. . . .
. . . .	. . . .	17.	. . . .	. . . .	. . . .	. . . .
. . . .	. . . .	18.	. . . .	. . . .	. . . .	. . . .

Comments: . . . . Comments at time of termination: . . .

. . . .

. . . . .Date . . . .

* Reprinted by permission from Ann Hardman, Southern Indiana Mental Health and Guidance Center, Jeffersonville, Indiana.

It may be appropriate for some consultees to fill out problem checklists independently while with others the consultant may ask questions to determine the areas in which individuals are having difficulties. For example, a teacher expressing difficulty in getting along with a certain student may be asked specifically, "How do you get along with other students, teachers, etc.?" to better determine the context within which problem situations occur, and with whom the most severe problems arise.

An example of an interview in which the consultant takes an inventory of problem behaviors is given below:

Teacher: These kids are driving me crazy.

Consultant: Sounds like they do a lot of things that bug you.

Teacher: Yes, they never bring their supplies, and they're always late for class.

Consultant: You've mentioned two areas of difficulty. I'm wondering if there are some other things they do that bother you.

Teacher: Well, they get out of their seats and talk out loud.

The consultant can be jotting down the teacher's responses to those questions. After identifying relationships in which s/he perceives a problem, the consultant can ask about situational events in which s/he may perceive problems. For example, s/he may say, "Tell me about some times when you have been really upset with these kids." In short, the consultant must attempt to identify the major problems and settings where the problem behaviors occur.

Select Concern for Consulting

If the consultee presents several problem areas, the consultant must begin to set priorities for treatment. There are four criteria which appear to be critical in making this determination (Sundel & Sundel, 1975). The first criterion is the problem of most immediate expressed concern of the consultee or significant others (family, friends, etc.). At this point, a profile of problems can be read out loud to the consultee or presented in a written list. The consultee can then be asked to select the problem that is of greatest immediate concern to him/her. For example, a mother may want her child to stop screaming. Some examples of what the consultant might say are: "Which problem is of the most immediate concern to you?" or "Which problem must you solve now?"

If the problem of greatest concern is possible to resolve quickly, it should be addressed first. If on the other hand, it is the most difficult problem and the one least likely to be resolved, it should be "shelved" and replaced by a more manageable difficulty. The success of changing one problem, even one which is not serious will provide some impetus and motivation for further problem solving.

A second criterion or way of determining a problem priority is to specify a problem which has the greatest negative consequences if not handled immediately. While a consultee may feel that a specific problem is of the greatest concern to him/her (e.g., being late for school), another problem may have greater negative consequences (e.g., dropping out of school, fighting). A consultee may feel that students should be on time or bring their own supplies but unless they attend more classes, they will be expelled from school. The consultant might ask the consultee what would happen if the problem were not resolved. Here, the consequences seem more severe for expulsion than for not bringing supplies or coming late and consequently warrant more immediate attention.

Averse consequences will be different for different people. Because individuals differ in their tolerance for the situation, examining the averse or negative consequences of the problematic behavior for the consultee and significant others provides a useful method for judging the intensity of behavior. For example, the degree to which the noisiness of Jerry's playing in the classroom becomes a problem is determined by the teacher who reprimands him. While one teacher may only be annoyed and ask him to "be quiet," another may find the noise intolerable and send him out of the room.

By examining what has happened in the past with the same people under similar conditions, the consultant and client can better predict the consequences of the consultee's behavior and weigh them accordingly. Some possible consultant statements might be:

What might happen if this problem is not resolved?
What happens after this specific behavior occurs?
What would likely happen to you if . . . . happened?

A third criterion for setting problem priority then is which problem can be corrected most easily, considering resources and constraints. What forces (people, situations) stand in the way of problem resolution? What resources exist that could help solve the problem? For example, a mother who feels trapped by her children may set going to school to complete an advanced degree as a goal but cannot afford a baby sitter and sees her husband's resistance as a further obstacle. Some possible consultant statements are:

What are some things that might prevent this problem from being resolved?

What are some things that will help you resolve this problem?

The last criterion for putting concerns in priority is related to the interrelationships of problem behaviors. That is, one set of behaviors may have to be dealt with before the specified problem can be solved. For example, it makes little sense to target academic behaviors (e.g., assignment completion, grades) if the child attends school infrequently. Likewise, before a child can learn to play with others, s/he must stop calling others names. The consultant might ask, "What would happen if this problem were solved?" Would the client make more friends, make better grades, feel better about him/herself?

Determine If the Problem Is Operationalized

Often the consultee expresses concern through the use of a label or labels. For instance, he or she may state feelings of "depression" or "nervousness," or a teacher may refer to a child as "rude" or "aggressive." While these labels offer a general indication of the problem area, they have different meanings for different people. Stated generally, then, they not only produce some confusion about the actual difficulty but are not amenable to evaluation.

Consequently, it is more beneficial to avoid labels and deal with specific behaviors which are observable and whose presence can easily be confirmed by two or more people. Examples of labeling rather than describing specific behaviors are as follows:

disruptive	rude	anxious
depressed	unmotivated	antisocial
aggressive	incorrigible	nervous

Exercise: Labeling

Directions: Indicate the problem statements that label behavior.

...... 1. Students won't respond when I ask them questions.

...... 2. I'm just miserable and figure there's no use in trying anymore.

...... 3. I'm really frustrated with my students.

...... 4. Bob gets out of his seat during discussions, talks out loud in class, and writes on other students' papers.

...... 5. Jack is an obnoxious show-off.

...... 6. Susan is a class clown.

...... 7. Bill is aggressive.

Answers: Labeling, 2, 3, 5, 6, 7; describing problem behavior, 1, 4.

It is typical for a teacher or parent who is referring a client, to use behavior labels, and it is useful for the consultant to allow them to speak of the problem behavior in their own terms. This will help establish rapport and at the same time, give the consultant a general idea of the type and range of problems experienced. After this has been done, however, the consultant should be able to determine if the behavior has been discussed in terms of labels or specific behaviors and if the former is the case, to be able to translate the label into behavioral terms.

When only behavior labels are used, the consultant really does not know the specific problem behaviors to be changed nor the behaviors which the client or referring person wants to promote. This obviously make the goal of consulting somewhat vague. On the other hand, a behavioral analysis specifies the undesirable behavior, helps elucidate some of the factors maintaining the undesirable behavior, and specifies the desirable behaviors which should replace the undesirable ones. This kind of analysis is closely related to treatment, then, because the goal is clear and the goal helps determine the best treatment approach.

In operationalizing the label, the consultant directs the client to give specific, concrete examples of behavior which led him to use the specific label he chose. For instance, if the consultee says the child is too shy, the consultant may ask for exactly what is meant, e.g., "Give me an example of what you mean by shy or describe a situation in which she was too shy." This proceeds until the consultant has a clear idea of what is meant by "shy." An example of operationalizing the label "too shy" follows:

1. Initiates no conversation with peers
2. Sits alone at lunch time
3. Holds head down and smiles when asked a question

An example of a behavioral translation in a consultant-consultee interchange is given below. The teacher is referring Johnny because of "disruptive classroom behavior."

Teacher: Johnny has been disturbing the whole class more and more — I just can't take any more of it.

Consultant: When you say Johnny disturbs the class, what do you mean? Does he get out of his seat, shout, throw spitballs? Can you give me a concrete idea of what he does?

Teacher: He usually starts a fight with someone near him.

Consultant: Uh-huh. Do you mean he hits someone close by, or starts a verbal argument over something?

Teacher: Well, he usually grabs something from another student or demands to see something on another student's desk.

Consultant: Good, I'm getting the picture now. When he does this, what do you do?

Teacher: Well, I used to be more patient, but now I get mad at him every time.

Consultant: Uh-huh, but what specifically do you do? Do you send him out of the room or go over to him and try to make him stop?

Teacher: I go over to his desk and tell him to stop it immediately, and if he is trying to grab something off a nearby desk, I pull it out of his hand and give it back to its owner.

Consultant: These details are important in understanding the situation better. Now, when Johnny isn't acting up, what do you do in regard to him?

Teacher: I try to get back to the rest of the class and hope that Johnny will do the lesson and pay attention.

Exercise: **Specific Behaviors**

Directions: For the following labels, substitute specific behaviors which are directly observable and can be validated by two or more persons.

1.   Uncoordinated: . . . .

. . . .

2.   Hyperactive: . . . .

. . . .

3.   Social isolate: . . . .

. . . .

4.   Devious: . . . .

. . . .

5.   Disruptive: . . . .

. . . .

Once the problem behaviors have been defined in behavioral terms and put in order of importance, the consultant must isolate those stimuli which precede and follow the problem behavior and serve to control its occurrence. That is, the consultant attempts to identify those stimuli which elicit problem behavior and specify the reinforcing or punishing stimuli which follow it. Often, controlling conditions evident in the stimuli directly preceding or following behavior either maintain the problem behavior or by some deficit in their operation fail to maintain the desirable behavior. For example, when a student grabs something off another student's desk, the teacher may go over to the first student's desk and ask him/her to stop it. Or a student may be trying to study but every time he opens a book he thinks of an argument he has had with his girlfriend. His thoughts are punishing, then, and prevent him from concentrating.

Determine When Behavior Occurs

It is sometimes difficult to specify antecedents that set the occasion for problem behaviors. By determining *when* the problem occurs the consultant can often detect what causes or at least what preceded the problem behavior. For example, a child may have temper tantrums only when mother is talking on the telephone. The time when the child has temper tantrums (while mother is on the phone) elicits or sets the problem off in this situation. Or the child may do poorly in math but not in reading or spelling. Questions such as: "When is she most negative?" "What time did she do this?" often can pinpoint when the problem occurs.

Determine Situation Where Problem Occurs

For some behaviors, the situation or the place where the problem occurs sets the problem off. In many cases these antecedent conditions are neutral stimuli which elicit involuntary behavior. For example, a bicycle may initially be a neutral stimulus for a child, but every time s/he climbs on it, some big kids threaten him/her and say they will take the bike. Thus, whenever s/he sees the bike, a fear reaction is elicited. Similarly, students who have had a negative test-taking experience may generalize this anxiety to all test-taking situations. For this reason, it is important to determine the situation in which the problem occurs. Questions such as "Where does this problem occur?" indicate the setting or location. By determining where the problem occurs, one can often identify the appropriate setting for intervention.

Determine What Precedes Problem Behavior

Some situations require detailed observations and analysis to determine what might be triggering the problems. For example, a child who does not get along with others may not be able to recognize social cues from others. When a group of children do not want a child to play with them, they may say, "We already have enough kids for the game" or "We've already started." Unless the child recognizes from these cues that children do not want him/her to play, s/he may enter the game in an inappropriate manner. Thus goals and planned intervention should assist him/her in recognizing the relevant social cues from the other children.

Under extreme conditions the antecedents (or what occurs before the problem behavior) may be affected by the consequences or what occurs following the problem behavior. For example, if a teacher or parent physically punishes a child each time s/he takes something (ball, pencil, game, etc.) from someone, the child may soon withdraw in the presence of the teacher or parent. Thus, if the teacher or parent were attempting to have the child interact with other children, his/her very presence may be in the way.

Questions such as, "What did he do before Bill shoved him?" or "What did you do before he got out of his seat?" can often pinpoint the antecedent conditions to the problem.

Determine What Follows the Problem Behavior

For operant behavior such as talking, thinking, and many motor reactions of the skeletal-muscular system, the controlling conditions are reinforcing or punishing stimuli. For example, when Bill cuts into line ahead of other children, he is positively reinforced by receiving his ice cream before others. Averse or punishing consequences might occur when Bill cuts into line and the teacher requires him to stay in the classroom during recess. Sometimes there can be both reinforcing and punishing consequences for the same behavior. In the above example, Bill may receive the ice cream cone (positive consequence) and then be sent home or reprimanded (negative consequence).

The consultant might gather information concerning what is maintaining the problem behavior with the following questions:

When is the problem most severe? least severe?
When do these situations occur?
How do the children respond to him/her after it happens?
What happens after the problem occurs?
What do you do after s/he does this?

Questions such as these often prompt the teacher or parent to examine what s/he is doing after the problem occurs. For example, a teacher or parent could be maintaining a child's aggressive behavior by criticizing when it occurs. When the child hits or kicks another child the teacher might yell, "Stop it," or make idle threats such as, "You know what will happen if you do that again." In most cases there are a number of factors which may be maintaining the problem.

In some cases the problem may not be determined by what precedes or follows the problem but by whether the client has the necessary skills to perform the desired behavior. For example, it may be that a child can recognize social cues, "We've already started," or "We've got enough kids on our side." S/he knows that the other children do not want him/her to play in this game, but s/he may not have the skills to ask them when s/he can play with them. Likewise, children may lack skills to start, maintain, or close a conversation. In the classroom the client (child) may not have the necessary skills to complete his/her assignments successfully. For example, most intellectual skills are arranged in hierarchical fashion (Gagne, 1970) where each skill is a prerequisite to the succeeding skill; a child may have trouble with long division because s/he lacks basic subtraction skills.

While some learning and social hierarchies have been empirically tested and are available, most hierarchies are determined by the situation. That is, in some cases a school system may provide a hierarchy of reading skills. By knowing which skills (e.g., comprehension) are difficult for a child the teacher could assess any prerequisite skills which may interfere with the ability to comprehend what s/he reads. In other cases the consultant must determine with the consultee what the prerequisite skills are. Questions such as, "What must the child need to know or do to respond appropriately in this situation?" are helpful. Prerequisite skills that are necessary to perform the desired behavior can then be stated in performance objectives.

Determine Who Owns the Problem

Once the problem and controlling conditions have been defined, it is important to identify anyone else other than the consultee who may be bothered by the problem. If others (employees, friends, relatives, supervisors, etc.) are bothered or affected by what the child is doing they are more likely to participate in the change (intervention) program. For example, the authors recently worked with a mother who had no control over her child. The child's uncle was also concerned about the child and allowed the child to shine shoes at his barbershop, *only* if he received a note each day from the child's mother saying that the child had come home from school on time and had completed his homework the preceding day. If either of these conditions were not met, the child was not allowed to work in the barbershop the next day. By involving more than one consultee in the change program, the consultant maximizes the possibilities for success.

It is important to know what the consultee has done to remediate the problem. First, the consultee may just wish to refer the client to a consultant without first doing anything about the problem itself. That is, a teacher may send a child to the school counselor-consultant because s/he keeps getting out of his/her seat. The problem is one that occurs in the classroom and needs to be solved by the teacher. Unless the teacher has tried to do something about the problem, the consultant may not know the severity of the problem or how committed the teacher is to changing it. Furthermore, if the teacher has tried to do something about the problem (e.g., reprimands, isolation) and it has not worked, the consultant needs to know this before setting goals and designing an intervention.

While the problems and controlling conditions may seem apparent, it is often advisable to verify these with the consultee. That is, it is important that the consultant and consultee agree on the problem and controlling conditions before additional data are collected. In some cases the consultant may think the consultee has understood the problem and its controlling conditions, only to find at the interview that s/he cannot restate the problem. The consultee may not be able to describe the problem at the interview either because s/he has not been listening or because s/he has distorted it. In either case, it is critical to reach an agreement on the problem and its controlling conditions so that the consultant and consultee will know where to collect additional data. The following questions could be used.

How would you describe the problem?
Do we agree that . . . . is the problem?
OK, so from what we have said what seems to be maintaining this problem?

Help Consultee Decide on Time to Work on Problem

The final step in the problem definition interview is to establish a time with the consultee to work on the problem. By deciding in advance on a time commitment, the consultant can determine if the teacher or parent is committed to working on this problem further. This prevents the consultant from spending valuable time collecting additional data only to find the teacher or parent is not interested in doing anything about the problem. By establishing a time, the consultant and consultee can also plan when they can work on the problem, thus, preventing other activities from interfering.

CONSULTING SKILLS INVENTORY

Directions: After each item, check YES or NO to indicate whether the skill has been demonstrated.

DEFINING THE PROBLEM		YES	NO
1.	Identify all concerns	. . . . .	. . . . .
2.	Select concern for consulting	. . . . .	. . . . .
3.	Determine if the problem is operationalized	. . . . .	. . . . .
4.	Determine when behavior occurs	. . . . .	. . . . .
5.	Determine situation where problem occurs	. . . . .	. . . . .
6.	Determine what precedes problem behavior	. . . . .	. . . . .
7.	Determine what follows the problem behavior	. . . .	. . . . .
8.	Determine who owns the problem	. . . . .	. . . . .
9.	Help consultee decide on time to work on problem	. . . . .	. . . . .

* * * * *

CRITERION TEST

Directions: Complete the following statements. Choose (a) (b) (c) or (d) where indicated.

1. The consultant can often determine what is causing the problem behavior by knowing
   - (a) the characteristics of the consultee
   - (b) the rate of behavior
   - (c) the time and place where the behavior occurs
   - (d) the goals

2. The consultant can often determine what is maintaining the client's behavior by asking
   - (a) What happens after the problem occurs?
   - (b) What happens before the problem occurs?
   - (c) Where does the problem occur?
   - (d) When does the problem occur?

3. In order to determine the easiest problem to treat, the consultant must ask
   - (a) Where does the problem occur?
   - (b) What sets the problem off?
   - (c) What forces stand in the way of the problem being solved?
   - (d) When does the problem occur?

4.   In order to determine the most immediate problem, the consultant might ask

  (a)   When does the problem occur?
  (b)   What would happen if this problem were not solved now?
  (c)   What do you think is causing the problem?
  (d)   Why do you think the problem is occurring?

5.   From the following referring problems below check those stated in behavioral terms.

  . . . . .   Bill is difficult
  . . . . .   Susie never follows directions
  . . . . .   Mary is lazy
  . . . . .   Frank never initiates a conversation
  . . . . .   Eric is hyperactive

6.   By asking the consultee to summarize the problem the consultant can

  (a)   establish agreement on the problem
  (b)   identify the problem
  (c)   set goals
  (d)   determine who owns the problem

Answers:

1.   (c)
2.   (a)
3.   (c)
4.   (b)
5.   Susie never follows directions; Frank never initiates a conversation.
6.   (a)

4

ASSESSING CLIENT BEHAVIOR

Assessment information helps to determine the level at which the problem is occurring and those events which are maintaining it. While it is assumed that this information will be collected, some decisions must be made concerning the methods of information collection as well as how it should be analyzed and who should carry out the assessment. Usually the consultant assists the consultee in making these decisions, but the consultee actually carries out the assessment. However, there are times when the consultant (or others) will carry out some or all of the above stated steps, once agreement has been reached by the consultant and consultee on the process and criteria (Kurpius & Lanning, 1975).

Determine How Assessment Will Be Carried Out

The first step in determining how the assessment will be carried out is to select the appropriate response characteristics of the behavior to be measured. Various types of assessment procedures are available and are differentially effective depending on the type of problem to be assessed. Basically, there are three broad areas which can be assessed: behavioral, cognitive and affective areas. Where the problems are clearly behavioral, they may be most accurately assessed through observations. However, where they are cognitive, standardized tests and work samples may be most useful, and where they are affective, self-report measures are often used. Each of these areas will be described in more detail below.

Make Behavioral Assessment

One of the most widely accepted ways of measuring client behavior is to record observations of the client in his/her natural environment (classroom, playground, back yard, kitchen, etc.). There are three major reasons why behavioral observations are efficacious.

55

First, specific problem behavior described by the consultee can often be assessed best through observation. For example, if a child shoves other children on the playground this can best be assessed through an observation. While checklists and verbal descriptions give evidence of difficulties, they are not as precise as actual observations and recordings of behavior.

Second, written goals and objectives can easily be derived from observational data. It is much easier to write a behavioral objective based on an observation that the child "interacts" positively with others one time per day than if fifty percent of the class say they do not want to play with the child.

Third, behavioral observations follow closely from the consultee's behavioral definition of the problem. Behavioral examples (hitting, initiating conversation, etc.) can be easily verified through recorded observations. In observing behavior, there are three attributes of client behavior which can be measured: frequency, duration, and intensity. Frequency refers to the number of times a behavior occurs, while duration is the length of time a behavior occurs, and intensity is the degree to which behavior occurs.

While there is no perfect measurement, the type of behavior under observation, the time available, and the setting in which it occurs determine how the assessment will be carried out.

Measure Frequency

Frequency is the most common measurement of behavior, and this may be recorded either by the actual number of times a behavior occurs or the rate at which it occurs. Behavior which is excessive (fighting) or deficient (not completing assignments) is most easily defined in terms of rate. Likewise, attendance, incorrect spelling of words, or complying with parental demands may be best expressed through rate or percentage. For example, if a parent were concerned about the rate at which children ignored parental demands, s/he might chart the behavior in this manner.

BEHAVIOR: NONCOMPLIANCE

Date	Time Observed	No. of Hours	No. of Target Behaviors	Rate
10/4	6:00-8:00 p.m.	2	4	
10/5	5:00-9:00 p.m.	4	9	
10/6	4:00-9:00 p.m.	5	15	

To compute the rate of behavior, divide the number of times a behavior occurs (frequency) by the amount of time. For the above data, the ratios would be 2, 2¼, and 3. If the observer has reason to believe that a behavior varies according to the time of day, s/he should record the behavior during the same time period each day.

The problem chart shown in Figure 4 has some usefulness for parents. As indicated on the chart, each parent can record the frequency of a given set of behaviors each day. By knowing what time the child woke up and when s/he went to bed, a response rate for each target behavior may be computed.

Figure 4: **Problem Recording Chart**

Child's name: ....   Age: ....

Behavior to be recorded:　(1)　Not following directions　(NFD)
　　　　　　　　　　　　　(2)　Name calling　　　　　　(NC)
　　　　　　　　　　　　　(3)　Arguing　　　　　　　　(A)
　　　　　　　　　　　　　(4)　Fighting　　　　　　　　(F)

Week beginning: ....

Week ending: ....

Instructions: Make a mark each time the problem occurs.

Monday	*Tuesday*	*Wednesday*	*Thursday*	*Friday*	*Saturday*	*Sunday*
NFD=	**NFD=**	**NFD=**	**NFD=**	**NFD=**	**NFD=**	**NFD=**
NC=	**NC=**	**NC=**	**NC=**	**NC=**	**NC=**	**NC=**
A=	**A=**	**A=**	**A=**	**A=**	**A=**	**A=**
F=	**F=**	**F=**	**F=**	**F=**	**F=**	**F=**

Recorded from:

....   a.m.

　　　　to

....   p.m.

Recorded by: ....

Measure Duration

Behaviors such as crying, studying or sleeping may be best measured by duration. However, sometimes the criteria for the occurrence of a behavior may include both frequency and duration. For example, the frequency of crying may be tallied, with crying behavior defined as "crying noise which lasts for five seconds or more." Similarly, it might be important to know that someone studies, but it is not as important as knowing *how long* that person studies.

In the following example, the consultant and consultee discuss a strategy for measuring a withdrawn child's behavior.

> Teacher: When other children play, he doesn't seem to want to take part.
>
> Consultant: Does he ever play with them?
>
> Teacher: Occasionally.
>
> Consultant: How often?
>
> Teacher: It's hard to estimate. Maybe once or twice a week.
>
> Consultant: How long does he play with them?
>
> Teacher: Sometimes he plays with them the entire recess period, but a lot of times he just walks off by himself.
>
> Consultant: I'm wondering if before next Monday you could record when he begins to play at recess and when he stops. On this chart, you might write what game he is playing and with whom.

Sample Chart:

Date: ....

Time Started Playing	Time Stopped Playing	Game: Participants

1. ....

2. ....

3. ....

4. ....

5. ....

6. ....

This chart provides not only the frequency, but the duration of time spent playing.

Specify Recording Procedures

Assuming that the consultant and consultee have decided to collect behavioral data and have determined what to observe and how to observe it, they must decide what kind of a recording technique to use. There are three principal ways to record behavior.

1. record evidence
2. record interval data
3. record sample data

At least one of these will be appropriate for a given client problem, and the particular method selected often determines whether or not the consultant or consultee will record the data.

Record Evidence

If the target behavior leaves evidence (e.g., incomplete assignments or an unmade bed), all that is required is a record and tabulation of the response. Incorrect problems on work sheets can be counted and the number of incorrect answers or percentage of incorrect answers shows the degree of the problem. Attendance, achievement test scores, percentage of problems not finished, number of homework assignments not completed, and pages of work not finished all measure low skill levels, low academic ability, or low motivation. In recording evidence, however, it is helpful for the parent or teacher to arrange for the child to have the same amount and kind of work each day, and to keep a record of unsatisfactory performances (number unsatisfactory/number assigned) each day for several days. This way, one day's performance can more accurately be compared with another day's performance.

Evidence is an inexpensive nonreactive measure. A nonreactive measurement is one which does not affect the way the client normally responds to a situation. For example, the presence of a consultant in a classroom or home may alter the typical behavior of the child. In order to reduce such contamination, then, the consultant might infer the child's on-task behavior from the number of assignments completed and the grades on those assignments. Similarly noncompliant behavior may be inferred from the number of dirty dishes left in the sink. The teacher, or parent in this case, could easily gather the data without the child's awareness that s/he is being observed. Remember that when a problem leaves evidence, the most appropriate person to record the data is the one (teacher, parent, coach, etc.) who is present when it occurs.

Exercise: **Evidence**

Directions: Given the following behavioral situations check those which leave evidence.

. . . . (a) assignments completed

. . . . (b) dishes washed

. . . . (c) attending behavior

. . . . (d) fighting

. . . . (e) food spilled

. . . . (f) property destroyed

. . . . (g) social interactions

. . . . (h) grades

. . . . (i) days tardy

. . . . (j) room cleaned

. . . . (k) achievement test scores

Answers: (a), (b), (e), (f), (h), (i), (j), (k)

Record Interval Data

For many behaviors, the easiest method of recording data is simply to count or tally the number of occurrences of the behavior during a given time interval. Each observation session is divided into equal time intervals and the observer records the occurrence or absence of a behavior during these intervals. In the illustration below, the observer recorded whether or not a student was on- or off-task during a two minute observation period. If the student was off-task at any point during each ten second interval, it was scored as off-task; otherwise, the student was scored as on-task.

+ — + — + + + — — + + +

+ = on-task
— = off-task

The interval size will generally vary from five seconds to one minute in duration, depending upon (a) the rate of the response and (b) the average duration of a single response (Gelfand & Hartmann, 1975). For high rate behaviors (e.g., behaviors which occur twenty to thirty times per hour), the interval should be sufficiently small so that two complete responses could not occur in a single interval. On the other hand, the interval should be at least as long as the average duration of a single response (e.g., out-of-seat). The use of excessively long intervals (e.g., five minutes) would obviously result in an underestimate of the frequency of the target behavior and might also result in an underestimate of behavior change as a result of a deceleration program.

In utilizing this procedure, a consistent method for observing behavior must be established. Target behaviors should be (a) counted on the basis of the proportion of the interval, e.g., a *yes* would be recorded if the behavior occurred during seventy-five percent of the interval, or (b) a *yes* would be recorded if the behavior occurred at any time during the interval. The latter method requires less judgment and thus is likely to be a more reliable method (e.g., two or more people are much more likely to agree on when the behavior occurs and does not occur).

Although interval recording provides a close approximation to either frequency or duration of the target behavior, the major disadvantage of this method is that it usually requires the undivided attention of the observer. If continuous recording places excessive demands on the parent or teacher, then the recorded observations will be unreliable (Wetzel & Patterson, 1975). Thus, if an interval recording is the preferred method of recording, the consultant would be the likely one to make the observation since the teacher may be unable to monitor the behavior as closely as necessary for this method.

Record Sample Behavior

If on the other hand, the consultant has little time to monitor behavior, then time sampling may be the preferred procedure. Time sampling is useful under two conditions. First, it is appropriate when the observer must record one or more behaviors of a single client or one or more clients. For example, if the teacher is working with several behaviors of one child, his/her record might show a sample of a different behavior for different times during a day. It is crucial to vary the time to sample each behavior in case the behavior may vary according to a specific time period (lunch, recess, etc.).

Secondly, time sampling is preferable when the problem behavior does not vary according to the time of day. For example, if a child gets out of his/her seat or talks out when s/he is hungry, this behavior would only occur at specific time periods (e.g., 11:00-11:45 a.m. and 2:30-3:15 p.m.). In this instance time sampling (i.e., recording at different times during the day) would not likely record this behavior; only interval or continuous recording would record when this behavior occurs most frequently.

Time sampling is a good method for recording behaviors which occur at very high rates (e.g., twenty to thirty times hourly, or low rates, e.g., five times daily) and last over a long period of time. For example, many behaviors are continuous, i.e., difficult to tell when they start or stop. It is possible, however, to record the presence or absence of such responses within a short time interval.

A variety of ways to count behaviors can be utilized, depending upon the rate of behavior. For low-rate behaviors such as fighting or enuresis, each event may be tallied as a complete event.

Example:

Name: . . . .   Date: . . . .

Observer: . . . .   Behavior: . . . .

Monday	1		1	1	1
Tuesday	1	1	1		1
Wednesday	1	1	1		1
Thursday	1	1	1		1
Friday		1	1	1	1

Time: 9:00-11:00   11:00-1:00   1:00-3:00

For high rate behaviors such as talking or playing with others, another approach may be necessary. One procedure is making one observation per unit of time and simply recording yes or no. That is, the consultant, teacher or parent might look at the child each fifteen seconds and record either the presence or absence of the target behavior at that specific point in time.

Playing with others	Seconds	15	30	45	60
	YES				
	NO				

If a single target behavior is being recorded (e.g., playing with others), the observer can make a tally mark or activate a wrist golf score counter to indicate each occurrence. If several behaviors (interaction behaviors, for instance) are under observation, however, a single letter can be used for each behavior (e.g., I = interactive play and P = parallel play). Regardless of the code used, it should be simple and easy to utilize.

The following dialogue illustrates how the consultant and consultee can decide on a recording method.

Consultant: So John doesn't complete his work.

Teacher: No, I know he's capable because he occasionally does it and his work is always above average. He just doesn't seem to care.

Consultant: It might be helpful to get an idea of just how often he does his work and whether or not there are differences according to the subject he's working on. Do you think you could keep a record of this?

Teacher: Sure, it would be easy since I usually write in my grade book anyway. (In this case, the easiest recording method would be evidence. Time on- and off-task could be used but would be much more time-consuming and would not offer enough additional information to make it feasible.)

Consultant: Suppose we make up a little chart. We'll write down the date and subjects and then you can check them as the assignments are completed. Put a (+) in the blank if the assignment is completed and turned in on time. If no assignment is given, put a (−) in the blank. It could look something like this.

Subjects

Date	Reading	Spelling	Math	Science	Social Studies
. . . . .	. . . .	. . . .	. . . . .	. . . .	. . . .

Teacher: Fine. That would be easy to record.

Consultant: This way, we can get an idea of about how many assignments are being turned in now. After you keep this record for a few days, we'll look at it and talk about some ways to increase his completion of assignments. OK.

Teacher: Sounds good. When do you want to see this?

Consultant: Do you have some free time on Wednesday?

In addition to frequency counts of specified behavior, an additional way to sample behavior is through some of the cognitive measures listed earlier. These are essentially work samples but they have the advantage of being given under optimal conditions. That is, they are often administered in a one-to-one situation (e.g., intelligence tests) where the examiner can prompt attending behavior and give frequent reinforcement.

Determine Where Observations Should Occur

Observations of the target response should occur *where* it occurs. For instance, undesirable mealtime behavior should be observed and recorded only at mealtime. Likewise, participation in games should be observed during recess or a free play period where the behavior is most likely to occur. In this regard, it is useful for the consultant to look closely at the pre-interview checklists and ask the consultee to observe where the problem occurs. If it occurs in more than one environment (classroom, home, etc.), an environment where the behavior occurs most frequently and where a consultee is present to treat the behavior should be selected.

Some problem behaviors occur only under highly controlled stimulus conditions. Such behaviors as table manners, fighting with peers, or numerous other social role behaviors often occur in specific environments and with certain people. That is, a person might fight only with select people (classmate, boy next-door, etc.). Thus, the target behavior might be observed where it occurs. Data can be sampled continuously throughout each period (basketball game, recess, etc.) or sampled for some segment of time within these periods.

Determine When the Observations Should Occur

There are several factors to consider in determining *when* to observe the target behavior. This depends on (a) the nature of the target behavior, (b) the nature of the treatment, and (c) various practical considerations such as the amount of observer time available and the extent and regularity of access to the child/client.

The nature of the target behavior and controlling conditions often determine when and where the behavior should be observed. Behaviors such as walking, thumb-sucking, and crying are not under tight stimulus control and occur almost any time of the day. Thus, these behaviors could be measured continuously (interval sampling) or by means of a time sampling procedure. Continuous observation would almost certainly require a consultant to make the observations since a teacher or parent would not have the time for such a procedure. For example, if crying occurred at home, a parent would likely be responsible for the observations and would likely use time sampling since it would require less time than continuous observation. Crying might be measured by detecting whether or not it occurs at any point during hourly periods.

Determine Who Should Make Observations

The consultee (parent or teacher) is *generally* the observer even though this depends upon *who* is present when the behavior occurs and how much time s/he has. For example, if fighting at recess is the target behavior, the teacher may be the most likely person to observe it. However, if the teacher is on recess duty, s/he may have other responsibilities, and maybe a teacher's aide would be the most appropriate person to make the observations.

Likewise, when/where the intervention is to take place will likely determine who makes the observation. For example, if a teacher is trying to teach social interaction skills during specific times in the week, s/he would be the most likely person to observe the interaction skills of the children. However, if the teacher were targeting academic behaviors all day, it would be impossible for him/her to make continuous observations, so the teacher's aide may wish to sample specific times or periods when the teacher is busy.

In general, the consultant should attempt to avoid recording behavior for three reasons. First, the consultant's mere presence may produce a novel situation and thereby change the child's behavior. (This is more likely to occur in the home than in the classroom, however, since a child is likely to be suspicious of a stranger who arrives at his/her home and observes his/her behavior.) Secondly, by recording data the consultant may be taking responsibility for the program away from the consultee. Thirdly, this is not an efficient use of the consultant's time. While s/he is recording data, s/he could be providing consultation services to others. It is recommended that the consultant only record behavior when observational recording cannot be done in any other way.

Make Cognitive Assessment

A common referring problem for the consultant is that of school difficulties or academic underachievement. Here, assessment is important in order to diagnose the problem area, to determine skill mastery levels, to assess proper academic placement, and to determine the most appropriate intervention. However, the responsibility for assessment may be shared by several people. For instance, the classroom teacher can collect work samples (classroom work in various subject areas) as well as observe and record behavioral data (number of assignments completed, time-on-task, etc.). The teacher can also record achievement test data. The school psychologist may be asked to collect data concerning intellectual ability, perceptual skills, and perhaps achievement; information on visual and auditory acuity (if appropriate) may be obtained from the school nurse and speech teacher, respectively. In addition, the learning disabilities specialist or reading teacher may be asked to administer diagnostic instruments to assess specific skills in reading, arithmetic and spelling.

In assessing the client's skills, both criterion-referenced and norm-referenced tests are used. Norm-referenced measures refer to a child's performance as compared to a norm group, either local, state or national. Having such scores, then, has the benefit of showing a child's learning relative to others but has the drawback of not giving specific feedback for instructional purposes. This is true particularly because a "good" item for a norm-referenced test is one which fifty percent of the students get right and the other fifty percent get wrong.

Criterion-referenced tests allow one to measure and describe a student's achievement with regard to a well-defined area of knowledge (Popham, 1974). They are based on a different approach to classroom instruction in which the subject matter to be taught is defined, broken down into units, specified in terms of instructional objectives, and evaluated according to mastery of the objectives.

The consultant's role in the assessment process requires that s/he understand both types of tests and be able to determine appropriate use of each type. The most typical norm-referenced tests are intelligence measures, and these have come under attack in the past few years because of the middle-class bias. It would be beneficial for the consultant to secure the American Psychological Association's 1964 publication, *Guidelines for Testing Minority Group Children* and become familiar with problems of norm-referenced intelligence tests as well as ways to accommodate for these problems. Additionally, consultants should become familiar with procedures for writing criterion-referenced test, e.g., Gronlund's *Preparing Criterion Referenced Tests for Classroom Instruction* (1973).

Achievement test data, both from norm-referenced and cri-terion-referenced tests, are useful. Norm-referenced tests help de-termine the particular age/grade level at which a child is working while criterion-referenced tests indicate particular skill mastery levels. Take the case of nine year old Bill, for example. Bill was referred by his teacher because his performance in reading and spelling was poor, he rarely finished his work, and he was easily distracted. The consultant first had a conference with Bill's teacher to gather in-formation and then she observed Bill in the classroom. She noted that Bill did not begin his work until five minutes after it was assigned, and that he stopped five times in a twenty minute period to talk with his peers. Following the classroom observation, the consultant had a conference with Bill's parents who indicated that his developmental history was normal and that his behavior at home was appropriate. Their only complaint was Bill's slowness in completing homework and his numerous excuses for not doing it. The consultant obtained recent and all past achievement test data as well as recent visual and auditory acuity information from Bill's cumulative folder. The school psychologist administered a WISC-R and Bender-Gestalt, and the learning disabilities specialist administered the Peabody Individual Achievement Test, Keymath Test, and Utah Test of Language Devel-opment. This data seemed adequate then to assess Bill's general learning aptitude and his mastery level in various subject areas.

Make Affective Assessment

Still a third area of assessment — that of affective behavior — may be signigicant in determining an appropriate intervention for a given client. This includes such areas as self-esteem, problem-solving or coping skills, and ability to get along with peers. Various standard-ized self-esteem instruments such as the Coopersmith and Piers-Harris are available, but the teacher may also infer self-esteem through the number of positive self-statements versus negative self-statements. Sociometric instruments (Cunningham, 1951) are helpful in deter-mining both perceived popularity of self in the classroom as well as actual popularity or peer acceptance and problem solving skills may be measured by an instrument such as Ojemann's Problem Situations Test or through observations of a child's response when angry or frustrated.

It should be noted, however, that even though several types of behavioral, cognitive and affective measures are described, only a few may be appropriate for a given client. When a referral is made, it will contain some description of the problem behavior. The consultant's role then is to determine what further information, if any, is needed and what types of measures would be most appropriate for obtaining that information.

Summarize Data

Behavioral data is more readily interpreted if it is recorded on prepared forms showing a tally for each time the behavior occurs. Included on this form should be the date, session number, child's name, observer, operational definition of the target behavior, times of observation, length of interval, and setting or activity. (See page 64).

Once the behavioral data has been recorded for several periods, graphing it is quite simple. Graphing can be done by either the consultant or consultee. If the consultee does not know how to graph behavior, the consultant can instruct him/her.

Consultant: OK, the first step is to draw two lines at right angles, one horizontal and one vertical, so that they meet at the lower left hand corner.

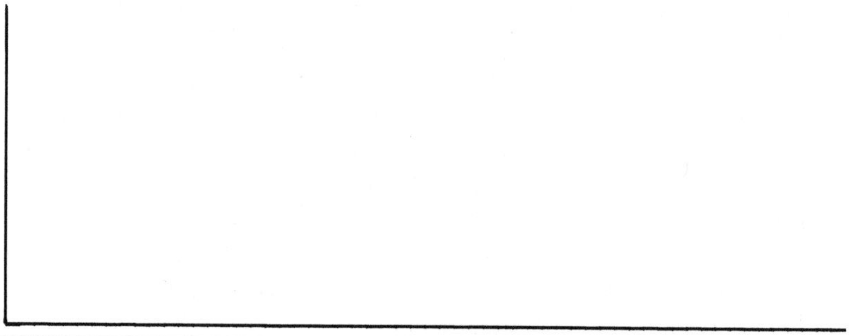

Figure 5: **Axis for Graphing Behavioral Data**

Teacher: OK, where do I record the data?

Consultant: Well, you enter the time of recording on the horizontal axis from the far left to the far right. Let me show you on this graph. You can enter days, months, minutes or whatever time period you're using here.

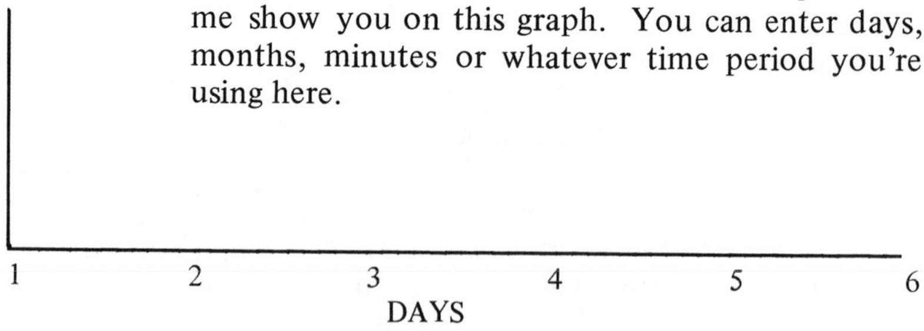

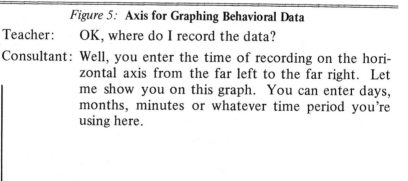

DAYS

Figure 6: **Axis for Graph with Recording Periods Entered**

Teacher: What goes on the vertical axis?

Consultant: Here we enter the number of target behaviors during the recording period.

Teacher: How do you know which numbers to use?

Consultant: This depends upon the maximum number of behaviors exhibited by the child per time period.
For example, on day 3, the maximum number of
behaviors observed were 10 and no other day was
greater than 10, so it would be the maximum number. The vertical axis would then be divided into
10 equal parts from 0 to 10, like this.

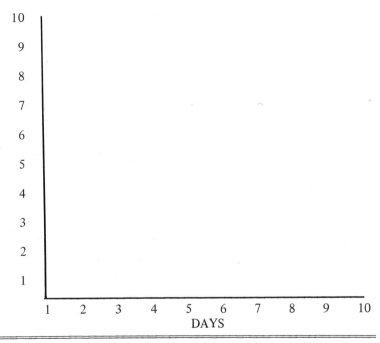

Figure 7: **Axes for Graph of Behavioral Data with Vertical Axis
Numbered and Labeled**

Teacher: I see. So then I enter the data for each day here.

Consultant: Yes, just enter a dot opposite the number corres-
ponding to the number of target behaviors observed
during that recording period. Then look at the
second recording period and enter a dot opposite
the number which tells the frequency of behavior
observed in that recording period. Just continue
until the data for each day are entered. When you
have plotted the data, connect the observation
points with lines, like this.

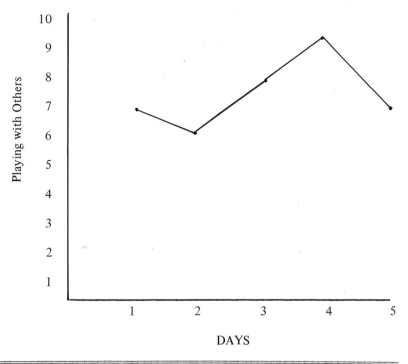

DAYS

Figure 8: **Axes for Graph Showing Plotted Behavior**

Exercise: **Measurement Units**

Directions: Examine the graph on the following page and then answer these questions:

1.   What is the unit of measurement in the graph? . . . .

2.   What is the length of time measurements? . . . .

3.   Given the following information, label the axis and plot the data on the graph.

       Will complied with parental requests 20% on Monday, 30% on Tuesday, 40% on Wednesday, 25% on Thursday, and 30% on Friday.

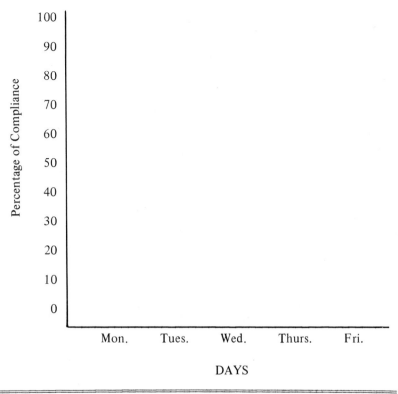

Figure 9: **Graph Showing Measurement Units**

Answers:

1. percentage of compliance

2. five days

3. graph on following page

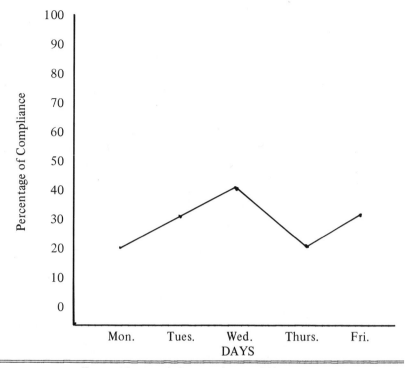

Figure 10: **Graph for Labeling and Plotting**

Once behavior is plotted on the graph, the consultant and client should determine whether the client's response rate is stable, i.e., whether or not it represents the typical rate at which the behavior occurs. If the baseline or pre-treatment data is characterized by extreme variation or a gradual increase or decrease, further observations should be collected until some stability is noted. Of course, these considerations must be weighed against the need for being treated; if the behavior is severely disturbing, treatment should supercede a stable baseline. Also, if too much time is spent collecting baseline data, it may require a cutback on treatment which is of greater importance.

Consultant: Let's look at the graph of Jerry's behavior and see if we can make any determination of his typical rate of noncompliance. It seems like his behavior is pretty stable except on Tuesday and Friday when he seems to be complying. What happens on those days that isn't happening on the others?

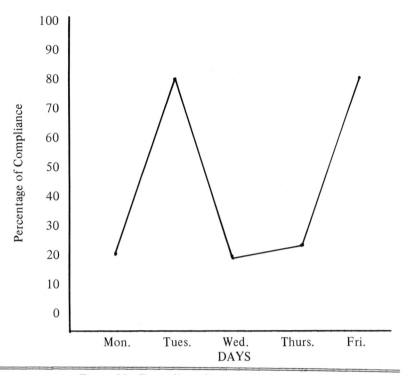

Figure 11: **Recording of Baseline Behavior**

Mother:	I'm not sure. I'm awfully busy those days. Mary is home from kindergarten so I spend less time with Jerry.
Consultant:	So maybe you make fewer requests of him
Mother:	Yes.
Consultant:	Let's look at your data sheets. It looks like that on those days, you make only four or five requests while on the other days, you make ten to fifteen. How many requests do you think it is reasonable to make each day?
Mother:	I guess maybe ten.
Consultant:	OK. That seems reasonable. Is there any reason why you couldn't continue to record his rate of compliance while you try to limit your requests to ten per day?
Mother:	I don't think that will be a problem, but I'm not sure why we should continue recording this.

Consultant: I understand your reservations about this, but if we know how often the behavior occurs, we can determine how much change to expect. Also, we might begin to determine what conditions are maintaining the behavior. For instance, right now the time and amount of requests may be controlling the rate.

Mother: I see. So you want me to keep everything the same so we can see what is controlling the behavior.

Consultant: Yes.

In some cases baseline data show a trend in behavior such as an increase or decrease, contingent upon particular conditions. For example:

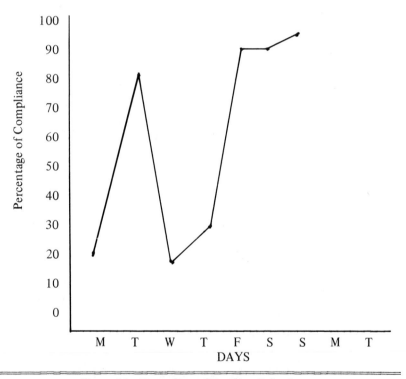

Figure 12: **Recording of Baseline Behavior**

Consultant: It seems that he is complying with your requests more often. Are you doing anything differently?

Mother: What do you mean?

Consultant: Something else may be going on that is modifying his behavior. Maybe he is aware you are keeping a record of his behavior or you may be responding differently to him when he complies.

Mother: I think he is aware that I am not asking so much of him. Maybe my tone of voice is different too. I used to tell him what to do in a very demanding voice. Now I think I am asking him.

Consultant: That could be making a difference. I don't think we need to do anything differently since he's complying more.

If a treatment program is initiated when undesirable behavior is decelerating, it will be impossible to determine whether or not the intervention itself was effective. That is, if the undesirable behavior is decreasing in the absence of treatment, then any further deceleration cannot be attributed solely to the treatment. Regardless, the consultant and consultee should attempt to sample enough behavior to establish some degree of stability.

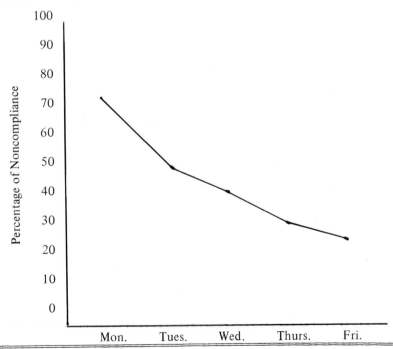

Figure 13: **Recording of Baseline Behavior**

Other data, e.g., the cognitive and affective data (as well as behavioral data) may be summarized on a form such as that shown in Figure 14 (Edge, Brown & Brown, 1979).

Figure 14: **ASSESSMENT DATA FORM**

Name .... Age .... Grade ....

Teacher ....

In each of the following areas specify both the weaknesses and strengths, if appropriate.

  I.   HEALTH
       Auditory acuity ....
       Visual acuity ....
       General conditions of health ....

  II.   COGNITIVE SKILLS
       Intellectual ability ....
       ....
       ....
       Reading skills ....
       ....
       Arithmetic skills ....
       Spelling and writing skills ....
       Language skills ....
       ....
       ....

  III. PERCEPTUAL AND MOTOR SKILLS
       Auditory perception ....
       Visual perception ....
       Visual-motor skills ....
       Fine motor skills ....
       Gross motor skills ....

  IV. COPING SKILLS
       Ability to solve problems ....
       ....
       Motivational level in the classroom ....

  V.   SELF CONTROL
       Attentional skills ....
       Ability to inhibit distractions ....
       General activity level ....

  VI. EMOTIONS
       Ability to handle strong emotions, e.g., anger ....
       ....
       Level of self-esteem ....

  VII. INTERPERSONAL RELATIONSHIPS
       Family relationships ....
       Peer relationships ....

Figure 14: **Assessment Data Form** – *continued*

SUMMARY

STRENGTHS: . . . .
. . . .
. . . .
. . . .
. . . .

WEAKNESSES: . . . .
. . . .
. . . .
. . . .
. . . .

RECOMMENDATIONS: . . . .
. . . .
. . . .
. . . .
. . . .

This form helps summarize strengths and weaknesses and points out areas to be remediated. It is particularly useful where the problem area is related both to academic as well as behavioral difficulties.

CONSULTING SKILLS INVENTORY

Directions: After each item check YES or NO to indicate whether the skill has been demonstrated.

ASSESSING CLIENT BEHAVIOR	YES	NO
1. Determine how assessment will be carried out	[ ]	[ ]
2. Make behavioral assessment	[ ]	[ ]
3. Specify recording procedures	[ ]	[ ]
4. Determine where observations should occur	[ ]	[ ]
5. Determine when observations should occur	[ ]	[ ]
6. Determine who should make observations	[ ]	[ ]
7. Make cognitive assessment	[ ]	[ ]
8. Make affective assessment	[ ]	[ ]
9. Summarize data	[ ]	[ ]

CRITERION TEST

Directions: Complete the following statements. Choose (a) (b) (c) or (d) where indicated.

1. Mike initated three conversations on Monday, two on Tuesday, four on Wednesday, five on Thursday, and one on Friday. What is his rate of initiating social interactions?

    (a)   10 per week
    (b)   4 per week
    (c)   3 per week
    (d)   3 per day

2. Time sampling is a preferred recording procedure:

    (a)   when intensity of the problem is in question
    (b)   when duration of the problem is in question
    (c)   when conditions prohibit continuous observation
    (d)   when evaluation is necessary

3. Data should be plotted on a graph because

    (a)   it illustrates a pattern of behavior often not found in a narrative
    (b)   it tests the reliability of the data
    (c)   it tests the significance of behavior change
    (d)   it provides nonvalid data

4. (a)   Given the following information, label the axis, and plot the data on the graph below.

        Eric was frequently fighting. On Monday he was in three fights, Tuesday in four fights, Wednesday in five fights, Thursday in three fights, and Friday in four fights.

    (b)   Should the baseline observations be stopped or continued? Why or why not?

5. The consultant usually is the observer
   (a) when the frequency of the behavior is recorded
   (b) when recording is continuous
   (c) when time sample recording is used
   (d) when evidence is recorded

6. List three attributes of client behavior that can be measured.

   (a) . . . .
   (b) . . . .
   (c) . . . .

Answers:

1. (c)

2. (c)

3. (a)

4. (a) graphed below

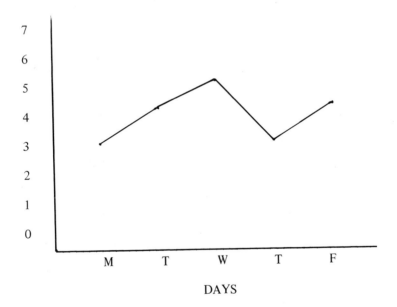

DAYS

   (b) stopped because the baseline is stable

5. (b)

6. frequency, duration, intensity

5

FORMULATING GOALS

The third chapter described how the consultant can help the consultee (teacher, parent) operationalize the problem This chapter is designed to help the consultant identify alternative desired behaviors that are incompatible with the problem behavior. That is, the third chapter focused on "what is" happening with the client while this chapter focuses on what the consultee " would like to see" happening.

Identifying the desired behaviors for the client can often be difficult for the teacher or parent. A parent may request help from the consultant-counselor in eliminating or decreasing problem behavior (e.g., temper tantrums, fighting), but may have given less thought to an alternative to fighting or tantrums. If the parent or teacher wishes to eliminate an undesirable attention-getting behavior, they must replace it with a desirable behavior which provides the child with an equal or greater amount of attention.

The process of identifying desired behaviors or goals provides a standard for where the consultant is going. Specific points along the way can be stated in the form of objectives to help the consultant and consultee measure their progress toward the goal. The effectiveness of consulting is measured by whether or not the consultee (teacher or parent) reaches the goals with the child (client).

Identifying General Goals

Desired behaviors or goals can be classified into three types: process, product and outcome. Process goals are related to the establishment of conditions necessary for consultee change, i.e., to therapeutic conditions which are chiefly the consultant's responsibility. These are general goals such as asking open-ended questions, paraphrasing and reflection of feelings. Such goals are generally considered universal in that they apply to all counseling or consulting relationships. That is, they refer to what the consultant does to encourage the consultee to talk about the problem, describe it in terms of specific behaviors, identify alternative desired behaviors, etc.

Product goals are the responsibility of the consultee. (S/he is responsible for doing something to alter the client's behavior and reaching his/her goals for the client.) The teacher may need to change his/her own behavior, e.g., design instructional materials, ask the child more questions, or praise the child each time s/he answers the question correctly. These behaviors should be stated in the form of objectives, and to the extent the teacher reaches his/her objectives, s/he will increase the likelihood that the child will reach his/her objectives. The product goals are interventions and are determined mutually (by consultant and consultee) only after the desired behavior has been identified for the client.

Desired behaviors or outcome goals are goals the consultee has for the client. They are goals which are directly related to the consultee's reason for seeking help. Outcome goals can be vague and imprecise, or they can be specific and precise. Regardless of their form, however, they must be goals the consultee can relate to and which s/he can accept as his/her own. Thus, it is critical that the consultant and consultee agree on the goals they hope to achieve.

Exercise: **General Goals**

Directions: In the following narrative, classify the goals according to Process, Product, and Outcome.

> The consultee is a mother who made an appointment to see the school counselor to get help for her son, Ted. Although the mother requested the interview, she had difficulty describing Ted's problem. The counselor-consultant attempted to reflect her feelings of inadequacy and asked many open-ended and probing questions to learn more about the mother's problem. The mother's problem seemed to be that Ted refused to comply with his parents' requests. Since the counselor-consultant wished to learn how often and when Ted refused to comply, he asked the mother to record each instance of noncompliance and what occurred before and afterward.

Objectives

Process: . . . .

. . . .

Product: . . . .

. . . .

Outcome: . . . .

. . . .

Suggested Answers:

Process: To use reflection, open-ended and probing questions in the interview.

Product: To have mother record Ted's noncompliance and what occurs before and after it.

Outcome: To increase Ted's compliance.

State Goals in Performance Terms

After goals are stated generally, it is helpful to translate these into specific behaviors which are measurable. That is, the consultant must determine from the consultee what behaviors the client will be performing in order to reach his/her goal.

The behavior to be encouraged by the consultee should be incompatible with the consultee's complaint. For example, a teacher complains that a child in his/her class is out of his/her seat all the time, and the teacher wants the child in the seat. In this case, the consultant should ask what the child should be doing at the seat (working on math problems, participating in a class discussion, etc.).

It is sometimes difficult for parents or teachers to describe what they want a child to be doing. The following transcript illustrates some of the problems of identifying desirable behaviors.

Parent: That's an understatement. I just want to read the newspaper and he is always doing something to annoy me.

Consultant: What does he do?

Parent: Well, last night he took all the coat hangers out of the closet and tied them end to end.

Consultant: What did you do?

Parent: I told him to pick them up or else I would send him to his room.

Consultant: What do you want him to be doing?

Parent: I just want him to stay out of things.

Consultant: Such as the coat hangers?

Parent: Yes.

Consultant: OK, you have told me what you don't want him to do. But what do you want him to do?

Parent: Well, I wish he would mind his business.

Consultant: What do you mean by minding his business?

Parent: Oh, maybe playing with his sister.

Consultant: What kinds of games could they be playing?

In the preceding example, the specified terminal behaviors describe what the child will be doing. Vague descriptions of the terminal behavior (e.g., minding his business) would not be acceptable since there would be no way to measure it reliably. For example, if the parent wants the child to "mind his business," what will he be doing? Working a puzzle? Playing a game?

In order to set attainable goals, it is important to know what resources the teacher or parent has at his/her disposal. In this example it would be important to know what games or puzzles the parent has available. Likewise, academic goals, by means of small progressive steps, might require that the teacher have programmed instructional materials available. In selecting a goal for what the child will be doing, it is crucial to consider whether the resources are available; and if they are essential but not available in the particular setting, they must either be obtained or replaced by alternative goals.

Exercise: **Objectives**

Directions: In the following exercise translate the general goals into specific operational objectives.

1. Reducing noncompliance: . . . .

2. Improving social relationships: . . . .

3. Improving self-concept: . . . .

4. Improving the child's attitude: . . . .

Possible answers:

1. The child will clean his room each time he is requested to do so.
2. The child will initiate more conversation with classmates.
3. The child will make more positive self-statements.
4. The child will attend to the teacher.

The tendency to set vague goals occurs frequently, simply because they are easier to name. Setting specific objectives, on the other hand, is a more difficult process. When teachers or parents have difficulty in describing desirable behavior, the consultant might ask: "What must he do to have a better attitude, to have better social relationships, etc.?" Answers to these questions often determine the consultee's goal.

Determine Conditions Under Which Behavior Occurs

Once the consultant and consultee have agreed on the goal, the next step is to specify the conditions under which the goal behavior will occur — when the behavior will occur, where it will occur, and across which situations. These conditions will often be situation-specific. That is, it may be easier for a child to interact with one child than a group of children. Likewise, it may be easier for a child to share materials with a brother than to share with a stranger. Each set of conditions may serve as a sequential step or objective toward reaching the desired behavior.

The conditions under which the behavior is to occur also helps to identify *where* the behavior is to occur. If a particular problem occurs at a certain place in the house (kitchen, living room, etc.), then this is where the desired behavior should occur. For example, if a child throws food at the dinner table, then the goal behavior (good table manners) should occur at the dinner table. Not only is this where the problem occurs, but it also makes it possible for the parents to monitor the child's behavior.

In some cases, parents or teachers may wish the goal behavior to occur across several situations. Parents may wish children to comply each time they make a request, regardless of location. Teachers are likely to want their students to complete all assignments accurately. Whatever the goal, however, the teacher or parent should be able to reliably measure desired behavior.

Specify Criterion Level for Behavior

Once the goal has been specified in performance terms and the setting in which the behavior is to occur has been identified, an acceptable level of performance must be established. The criterion level refers to the frequency and/or quality of the behavior. For example, "completion of assignments" is not a useful indicator of successful performance of desired behavior because it does not tell if the child should complete *all* assignments, fifty percent, twenty-five percent, or whatever. It is more helpful to indicate the desired level, e.g., completing eighty percent of all assignments for the next week. In this case, the consultant and consultee will know when the goal is reached.

In determining criterion levels of success, it is important to know how well the client is now performing. Goals which are unreasonable will likely fail. Consequently, only achievable goals should be set and these can be based on the client's current performance level.

For instance, if the client is now failing all classes, it would be unreasonable to set a goal of straight A's. Rather, it would make more sense to set a goal of earning all passing grades or possibly grades no lower than C's. Similarly, a more reasonable initial goal for a withdrawn child would be doubling the number of times s/he participates in a class discussion rather than having her/him lead a discussion. Likewise, a reasonable first goal for a child who is completing twenty percent of the assignments in math would be to aim at fifty percent completion rather than ninety percent or one hundred percent completion.

Achievable goals should be set for teachers also. A teacher who never praises his/her students might set a goal to praise them four times an hour rather than once every five minutes. Reasonable criteria levels refer to what can reasonably be accomplished in the near future. Then, once a goal is reached, it is possible to specify a new goal and select the procedure appropriate to its attainment.

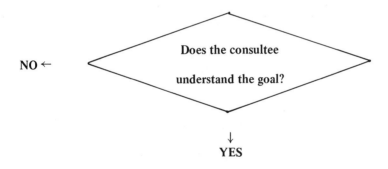

NO ←   **Does the consultee understand the goal?**

↓
YES

A common error that consultants make is assuming that the consultee understands the goal. This often occurs when the consultant fails to summarize or ask the consultee to summarize what was helpful in the interview. Effective goal setting can be measured by having the consultee restate the goal (Vriend & Dyer, 1974). Simply agreeing with the consultant is not enough because the consultee may leave with a very different interpretation of the goal than that of the consultant. If distortions do occur, these can be identified in the restatement and then be dealt with.

One way to avoid distortions and also to establish measurable goals is through the use of goal attainment scaling. This procedure (Kiresuk & Sherman, 1968) involves three basic steps and ends with a written product mutually agreeable to the consultant and consultee.

These steps are:

1. *State the goals behaviorally.* These may be either process, product or outcome goals but should be stated clearly and should be decided on mutually by the consultant and consultee. These goals may become evident by answering the question of what behaviors need to be changed and what should replace them.

2. *Weight the goals.* Some goals are obviously more important than others so they should be weighted to show their comparative value. These weights are assigned rather arbitrarily and may take the form of 1 - 5 value, with 1 referring to least important and 5 referring to most important. It should be noted that it is the relative or comparative rather than the absolute weight, that is significant. If all goals are equally important, they will be assigned the same weight, probably 1.

3. *Assign levels of expected attainment.* In this phase, the consultant and consultee specify five levels of possible outcome in relation to each goal. These outcomes have a progression of attainment, including: (a) most favorable treatment outcome thought likely; (b) less than expected success; (c) expected level of success with intervention; (d) more than expected success; (e) most favorable outcome thought likely.

Figure 15 on the following page shows a completed goal attainment record. Note that these goals are stated in performance terms and specify the criteria for success. Consequently, measurement is relatively simple and evaluation of goal attainment is straightforward.

Teachers and parents sometimes resist goal setting because they feel the situation is hopeless and cannot be changed or are unwilling to put forth personal effort (Tharp & Wetzel, 1969). Resistance may take the form of verbal wandering (discussing irrelevant topics) or looking for easy alternatives, ignoring the probability that the easy alternatives will not work. This typically happens in the early phases of consultation, perhaps in what Berlin (1964) calls the "honeymoon phase" of consultation.

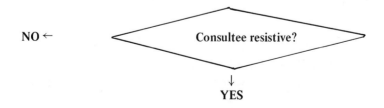

Figure 15. **GOAL ATTAINMENT RECORD**

Goals and Weights

Follow-up Date . . . .

Attainment Levels	Completion of Assignments	Interpersonal Skills	Compliance
		Weight = 1	Weight = 1
A. Most unfavorable outcome thought likely	Weight = 1 Completes no assignments	Has negative interactions with peers	Refuses to comply with any requests
B. Less than expected success	Completes 55% or less of assignments	Interacts positively with peers no more than once or twice per week	Does as told after first request 40% of time
C. Expected level of success with intervention	Completes 80% of assignments	Interacts with peers positively at least 3 times per day	Does as told after the first request 70% of the time
D. More than expected success	Completes 90% of assignments	Interacts with peers positively as often as 5 times per day	Does as told after the first request 80% of the time
E. Most favorable outcome thought likely	Completes all assignments	Interacts with peers as often as 5 times per day and has at least one after school contact per week	Does as told after first request 90% of the time

During this "sizing up" time, both the consultee and consultant are often trying to make good impressions and are not dealing with some of the basic problems. For instance, the consultee may be expressing appreciation to the consultant for help, but then later is saying frankly to a colleague that s/he thinks the consultant is unrealistic about school settings and really cannot help. If the consultant can become aware of underlying feelings and bring these out, reacting to them in a nondefensive manner, the working relationship will be improved and will produce better results. For example, Ms. Jefferson, the consultant noted Mr. Wayne's frown when the suggestion of classroom observation came up. Instead of going on with the discussion, Ms. Jefferson said, "How do you feel about observation? I'm sure there are other ways to get this information if observation presents a problem." Mr. Wayne responded that, "The observation would be fine, but I'd really feel pressed to do it myself. There are so many things going on in my room that I can't easily get free to observe for a period of time or even to jot down things while I'm teaching." Because Mr. Wayne expressed his reservations, it was possible to get someone else to observe. Otherwise, the teacher may have agreed to do it and never have followed through.

A similar issue the consultant should be aware of is the consultee's feeling of failure in not being able to handle a particular problem. In such a case, the consultee may think that if the consultant's suggestions also fail, his/her inability to change the child is not a failure on his/her part, but that the child in the classroom is just especially difficult. For this reason, it is important that the consultant show understanding of the difficulty the teacher is having with the child and not appear judgmental or critical of the teachers's procedures. This will help decrease the resistance and make the consultee more willing to try things and to honestly encourage success.

Another common reason for resistance is the consultee's belief that the intervention will require a great deal of time. In exploring this resistance, the consultant might discuss the amount of time the consultee currently spends with the problem behavior. If the teacher is currently spending an excessive amount of time with the child s/he may be less resistive to carrying out an intervention which would also be time-consuming.

Goals Acceptable to Consultant and Consultee?

If the consultee is not resistive or if the resistance has been dealt with, the goals should be agreed upon by both the consultant and consultee. While the consultee should actively participate with the consultant in formulating goals, there are times when the consultant may not agree with the consultee's goals. For example, while decisions about children's behavior are the responsibility of parents or teachers, these decisions may serve the interests of the parent or teacher rather than the child. A mother may wish that her son stay in the bedroom so he will not bother his father while he reads the newspaper. A teacher may wish that a child stay in her seat and be quiet, even though the child has nothing to do. In each of these instances the teacher or parent is likely to be concerned about his/her own interests rather than the interests of the child.

The consultant in these cases must ask whether the goals are likely to ultimately benefit the child or if they are reasonable expectations for children. The consultant and consultee should discuss how each goal will contribute to the child's academic and social development.

Decide If Consultant Can/Will Handle the Goal

Once the consultant and consultee have decided on an acceptable goal, the consultant must decide whether s/he has the knowledge to handle the case and if s/he is willing to do so. When the consultant lacks the requisite knowledge to carry out a goal, it is important that s/he not steer the consultee toward such a goal. In such a case, although the consultant may provide some initial help, the *real* problem will often still exist. For example, the consultant may be able to help a teacher design an intervention to keep a retarded child in his/her seat, but unless the proper curriculum is provided, the child will not achieve academically.

There are several things a consultant can do to decide whether s/he has the necessary knowledge to help the consultee reach his/her goals. First, consultants may wish to contact other professionals who have skills in a special area (marital counseling, retardation, etc.). In some cases, these specialists may offer to serve as a backup or supervisor to the consultant. While the consultant works with the consultee, s/he may receive assistance from the specialist.

A second inexpensive way for the consultant to assess her/his knowledge would be to complete the many self-instructional texts available on the market. For example, Becker, Engleman & Thomas provide self-instructional texts on classroom management (1974) and instruction on the learning process (1975). Gelfand & Hartmann (1976) have recently published a self-instuctional text, *Child Behavior: Analysis and Therapy*. Each of these texts will help the consultant assess his/her knowledge of specific techniques.

CONSULTING SKILLS INVENTORY

Directions: After each item check YES or NO to indicate whether the skill has been demonstrated.

FORMULATING GOALS	YES	NO
1. Identify general goals	. . . . .	. . . . .
2. State goals in performance terms	. . . . .	. . . . .
3. Determine conditions under which behaviors occur	. . . . .	. . . . .
4. Specify criterion level for each goal behavior	. . . . .	. . . . .
5. Determine whether goals are acceptable to consultant and consultee	. . . . .	. . . . .
6. Decide if consultant can/will handle the goal	. . . . .	. . . . .

* * * * *

CRITERION TEST

Directions: Complete the following statements. Choose (a) (b) (c) or (d) where indicated.

1. An example of setting an acceptable criterion for goal performance is:

    (a) The teacher will praise the child each time s/he shares a toy with a classmate.
    (b) The teacher will praise the child when s/he raises his/her hand.
    (c) The mother will praise her son when he is playing quietly with his sister.
    (d) The mother takes the children to the movies when they finish the dishes.

2. Which of the following goals might be unacceptable to the consultant?

    (a) reduce fighting by eighty percent for one week
    (b) always avoiding children who tease
    (c) completing all assignments for the next week
    (d) complying with parental requests eighty percent of the time

3. Given the following goals, indicate whether each is a *process*, *product*, or *outcome* goal.

    . . . . The consultant will attend to the consultee during a thirty minute interview eighty percent of the time.
    . . . . The consultee will smile each time the child completes an assignment.
    . . . . The child will arrive at class on time for one week.

4. Of the following objectives, which is stated in behavioral terms ?
   (a) be able to reduce anxiety
   (b) be able to complete more work
   (c) be able to reduce fighting
   (d) be able to have more self-respect

5. Statements of performance objectives include three pieces of information:
   (a) percentage, frequency and conditions
   (b) performance, percentage and location
   (c) performance, location and time
   (d) performance, conditions and criterion

6. Given the three basic criteria for an adequate performance objective, indicate which objective meets all the criteria.
   (a) The student will arrive in class on time frequently.
   (b) The student will show a ten point increase on a prespecified self-concept measure by the end of the month.
   (c) The student will show a twenty percent decrease in anxiety by the end of the week.
   (d) The student will show an increase in assignment completion.

Answers:

   1. (a)
   2. (b)
   3. process, product, outcome
   4. (c)
   5. (d)
   6. (b)

DESIGNING THE INTERVENTION

Once general goals and objectives have been established for the client and all the assessment information has been collected, the consultant and consultee are ready to design the program. The first step in this process often involves the consultant and consultee reviewing information which might be useful in examining alternative solutions and a method for delivery.

Review Information

Pertinent information usually consists of observations, interview data, rating scales, and normative and criterion test data. This information usually helps the consultant and consultee determine those events which both encourage and discourage the child's behavior. It also helps them make an adequate assessment of the problem behavior. A sample transcript follows:

Consultant: Let's take a look at what we have there. We agreed that things would be better if Jack stayed in his seat, talked out less, and completed more assignments. Let's look at the information and see if we can figure out what might be reinforcing this behavior. Are there times when he seems to be working harder than at other times?

Teacher: Well, from this graph, it's a little hard to tell. It seems that on Monday and Wednesday, he is better.

Consultant: What happens on those days?

Teacher: Well, I have another reading group then and Jack is doing seat work.

Consultant: So, it's difficult on those occasions to attend to Jack's good behavior.

Teacher: Hmm.

Consultant: It also seems that the children encourage Jack's behavior.

Teacher: Yes, I'm surprised. I hadn't noticed that.

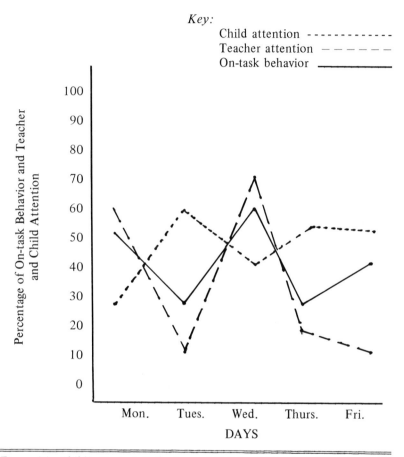

Figure 16: **Child's On-task Behavior and Child and Teacher Attention**

The advantage of looking at graphed behavior is that it provides a vivid illustration of what might be controlling a child's behavior. Notice that the consultant made no judgmental statements about the graph since this would likely bias the consultee. It is important to know how the consultee interprets the data to attain an estimate of commitment and knowledge of the problem. Subtle comments and many nonverbal behaviors that are not noticed by a teacher or parent can be detected through systematic observation.

> Consultant: Are you in a position to see Jack when you are teaching your reading group?
>
> Teacher: No, I generally don't notice what is going on in the other part of the room unless there is a noise.
>
> Consultant: So on Monday and Wednesday when Jack is in your reading group, he is in his seat working but on the other days when he is working independently, the other children encourage his misbehavior.
>
> Teacher: It seems that way.

By focusing on factors controlling the client's problem behaviors, the consultant and consultee increase the likelihood that the intervention plan will be successful. In the preceding example, attention from other children maintains Jack's behavior. If attention encourages undesirable behavior, then it can be used to encourage desirable behavior as well.

Once consultant and consultee have examined what might be reinforcing Jack's off-task behavior, the next step is to identify those events which might reinforce or encourage on-task behavior. In this case, the consultant and consultee must identify reinforcers which are stronger than those which the client is receiving for his present undesirable behavior. In the above example we know that teacher attention is reinforcing for Jack but it may be *more* reinforcing for Jack to talk to someone or have others laugh at his jokes than to receive the teacher's praise for desirable academic behavior. While the consultant and consultee should attempt to incorporate existing events (attention, recognition, etc.) which may be encouraging Jack's behavior, it is also crucial to identify factors which might influence his behavior. These are often events (games, food, etc.) which the consultant and consultee have not observed the client engaging in. Reinforcement rating scales can be used to determine the value that these events have to the client. (See Table 5.)

> Consultant: OK, it seems like we need something for him to work with on Tuesday, Thursday and Friday. Let's take a look at the rating scale. He really seems to like UNO.
>
> Teacher: Oh, yes, he really is enthused when someone brings a game to school. I didn't know he liked UNO.
>
> Consultant: When do you let him play with the games?
>
> Teacher: Generally at recess or the last hour on Friday.
>
> Consultant: I wonder if UNO couldn't be something we could use to encourage his good behavior.

Table 5: **Reinforcement Rating Scale**

How much pleasure does each of these items give you? Check the applicable column.

Item	Not at all	A little	Some	Much	Very much
1. Food					
(a) Candy	. . . . .	. . . . .	. . . . .	. . . . .	. . . . .
(b) Fruit	. . . . .	. . . . .	. . . . .	. . . . .	. . . . .
(c) Ice cream	. . . . .	. . . . .	. . . . .	. . . . .	. . . . .
(d) Nuts	. . . . .	. . . . .	. . . . .	. . . . .	. . . . .
2. Games					
(a) UNO	. . . . .	. . . . .	. . . . .	. . . . .	. . . . .
(b) Monopoly	. . . . .	. . . . .	. . . . .	. . . . .	. . . . .
(c) Checkers	. . . . .	. . . . .	. . . . .	. . . . .	. . . . .
(d) Bingo	. . . . .	. . . . .	. . . . .	. . . . .	. . . . .
3. Reading (books)					
(a) Adventure	. . . . .	. . . . .	. . . . .	. . . . .	. . . . .
(b) Mystery	. . . . .	. . . . .	. . . . .	. . . . .	. . . . .
(c) Comic	. . . . .	. . . . .	. . . . .	. . . . .	. . . . .
(d) Sport	. . . . .	. . . . .	. . . . .	. . . . .	. . . . .
(e) Biography	. . . . .	. . . . .	. . . . .	. . . . .	. . . . .
(f) Car	. . . . .	. . . . .	. . . . .	. . . . .	. . . . .
4. Activities					
(a) Jumping rope	. . . . .	. . . . .	. . . . .	. . . . .	. . . . .
(b) Kickball	. . . . .	. . . . .	. . . . .	. . . . .	. . . . .
(c) Basketball	. . . . .	. . . . .	. . . . .	. . . . .	. . . . .
(d) Swimming	. . . . .	. . . . .	. . . . .	. . . . .	. . . . .
(e) Baseball	. . . . .	. . . . .	. . . . .	. . . . .	. . . . .
5. At Home					
(a) Watching TV	. . . . .	. . . . .	. . . . .	. . . . .	. . . . .
(b) Staying up late	. . . . .	. . . . .	. . . . .	. . . . .	. . . . .
(c) Playing outdoors	. . . . .	. . . . .	. . . . .	. . . . .	. . . . .
(d) Inviting friend to spend night	. . . . .	. . . . .	. . . . .	. . . . .	. . . . .
(e) Listening to records	. . . . .	. . . . .	. . . . .	. . . . .	. . . . .
6. At School					
(a) Cleaning blackboard	. . . . .	. . . . .	. . . . .	. . . . .	. . . . .
(b) Feeding pets	. . . . .	. . . . .	. . . . .	. . . . .	. . . . .
(c) Teaching lesson	. . . . .	. . . . .	. . . . .	**Much .**	. . . . .
(d) Leading line	. . . . .	. . . . .	. . . . .	. . . . .	. . . . .
(e) Sweeping floor	. . . . .	. . . . .	. . . . .	. . . . .	. . . . .

Notice here that the consultant only discussed what might be reinforcing to the child. By questioning whether games and attention are events which might influence Jack's behaviors, the consultant has provided the consultee with the opportunity to accept or reject reinforcement as a means for influencing client behavior.

If the consultee is not agreeable to using something to reinforce the child's good behavior, then an alternative approach must be used. Some resistance may arise at this point. For example, the consultee may feel that the use of rewards to encourage good behavior constitutes "bribery." That is, the consultee thinks the child should do the work because it is his/her responsibility. The teacher might say, "No one ever paid me for being good." or, "He is able to do it on Monday and Wednesday, so he should be able to do it on the other days." In this case, the consultant might remind the teacher that his/her behavior is reinforcing to the child on Monday and Wednesday but that the children are reinforcing the child's off-task behavior on the other days. In general, the consultant can explain that bribery refers to being "paid off" for undesirable behavior. When people are paid off for desirable behavior, it is usually referred to as salary, commission, approval, etc.

In some instances, a teacher may prefer aversive control. This often occurs when the teacher is "angry" with the child and would rather control behavior with punishment than reward. Unfortunately the intended punishment is often reinforcing to the child. For example, the teacher may scold a child's undesirable behavior and the child is happy because being scolded is the only way s/he can receive attention. However, the major problem is that punishment is often more reinforcing to the teacher because it suppresses the level of undesirable behavior temporarily. Unfortunately, the results of punishment are not always long-lived and it does not specify the behavior which *should* occur.

In the case of Jack, the teacher does not seem to be punishing Jack's behavior. If the teacher shows no preference for this procedure or shows no other form of resistance, the consultant can begin the next step of the consulting process.

Design a Plan

After identifying those events which both encourage and discourage desirable goal behavior (staying in one's seat, completing assignments, etc.), the consultant and consultee can decide how the program will be carried out. This usually involves agreement on a set of procedures, the time, and the individual responsibilities for implementing the program.

This is a critical stage in the consultation program because a number of impeding factors often arise in the consultation relationship. First, the teacher or parent may still have unrealistic perceptions of the consultant role. Even though the consultant may have explained his/her role (see Chapter Two), the consultee may still expect the consultant to assume responsibility for the program. That is, consultees often expect the consultant to do both the planning and implementation of the program. Simply explaining the limits to the consultee at the outset is often not enough. However, if the consultant has discussed his/her role earlier, it will be much easier to redefine the limits of the program later than if s/he just "drops it" on the consultee during the program. Regardless, the consultant must always remind the consultee that s/he is interested in providing support but that s/he will not assume responsibility for the client's behavior. The following transcript indicates how the consultant might handle the problem.

Teacher: Well, I'm not sure I have time to give Jack this much attention. Why don't you work with him?

Consultant: I won't be able to do that for you. Remember when we discussed my role earlier. Maybe we can think of some ways that will require less time from you.

In many cases, the consultee wishes that the consultant would assume responsibility because s/he is bothered by the costs in terms of time and/or effort. In this case, the consultant can remind the consultee of their earlier agreement but also can discuss how the time can be reduced.

The time problem, as well as other reasonable issues, can be dealt with through problem-solving. The problem-solving process is based on four assumptions: (1) There are a number of potentially effective ways to handle a problem. (2) Teachers or parents are often aware of some alternative ways to alter a problem. (3) There is a greater likelihood of selecting the most effective solution among these various alternatives. (4) Teachers or parents will more likely implement a solution if they suggest it. When the consultant and consultee generate alternative solutions, it helps the consultee to take greater "ownership" of the intervention program, and the consultee is less likely to say "yes, but" to the consultant's suggestions.

Generate Alternative Solutions

Generating alternative solutions is central to the problem-solving process, with the goal of identifying as many potential solutions as possible. The end result, hopefully, will be that some of the solutions, or modifications thereof, will be acceptable to both consultant and consultee.

In generating alternative solutions, the consultant and consultee use a "brainstorming procedure." There are three basic rules for good brainstorming. First, criticism is eliminated. If the consultant or consultee suggests an alternative solution (e.g., "maybe I would arrange the chairs in a U formation"), each party refrains from criticizing. Secondly, the consultant and consultee can take an idea and improve on it. For example, the teacher might suggest, "I could praise him for interacting positively with others." The consultant in turn might suggest, "Maybe your praise can also tell him why you are praising him." Finally, both parties should attempt to generate as many solutions as possible. The greater number of possible solutions generated, the more likely an effective solution will be found.

At this stage, it is not necessary to state the alternatives in behavioral terms. Trying to clarify the meaning of a solution will often conflict with the "free wheeling" or the "brainstorming" nature of generating solutions. Later, after consultant and consultee have decided on the "best" solution, they can decide on how to carry out each step.

The consultant may introduce problem-solving in the following manner:

Consultant: OK, we have identified some reinforcers that Jack might prefer so let's think of some ways that those could be delivered. There are likely disadvantages and advantages for each strategy but we could discuss those later.

The following transcript also illustrates this procedure:

Consultant: We seem to have a clear picture of those things that might encourage and discourage Jack's behavior. Let's see if we can think of some ways to handle the situation.

Teacher: Well, I could let him go to the game area when he has finished his work, but then everyone would want to go.

Consultant: OK, that's one way to encourage him to finish assignments. We'll discuss the limitations of each later. What are some other possibilities?

Teacher: Maybe I could let him go to the library when is finished. The library has several games that he likes to play.

Consultant: Fine. Anything else?

Teacher: No. I can't think of any others.

Consultant: Whom would he play with?

Teacher: Well, I guess other kids who have work finished.

Consultant: Hm. Let's look at the advantages and disadvantages of each of these possibilities.

If the consultee is having difficulty generating solutions, the consultant can present some case studies describing solutions to similar problems. Or, s/he can generate alternatives along with the consultee. This sometimes occurs when special knowledge is required (e.g., designing a social skills program) to meet the performance objectives. Nevertheless, the consultant should make every effort to elicit alternative solutions from the consultee. If the consultee suggests a solution to the problem, s/he will be more likely to carry through with it. After enough solutions have been generated, they can begin to discuss the advantages and disadvantages of each.

Evaluate Each Solution

In specifying advantages and disadvantages of each solution, the consultant and consultee are assessing cost-effectiveness. What is the *best* solution for the client for the *least* amount of cost to the consultee?

Teacher: I think if I send Jack to the library, it would be better than letting him play in the classroom. Then everyone would want to play games in the room.

Consultant: The advantage would be to keep everyone from wanting to play games. It seems though, that the library might be a more rewarding place then the classroom.

Teacher: What do you mean?

Consultant: Well, if the fun things go on in the library rather than the classroom, he would rather be in the library.

Teacher: OK, but how do I handle the other kids when he goes?

Consultant: Let's think of ways to handle that. Could others who complete their work have an opportunity to play games?

Teacher: Where would they play? I just don't have the room.

At this stage, the benefits to the child (advantages) are pitted against costs in time and materials (disadvantages) to the teacher. In this case, only the consultee can make a proper comparison after the discussion.

Consultant: If you had the room, would this be a possibility?

Teacher: Sure, I wouldn't mind giving students free time if they have completed their work.

Consultant: Are there any areas not being used by the students?

Teacher: Only where the cabinets are.

Consultant: What do you normally keep in them?

Teacher: Usually the students' workbooks and macrame materials.

Consultant: Is there any other place that you could put them?

Teacher: Well, I guess the children could keep their workbooks. I could put the macrame materials in my desk.

While giving the teacher ideas to implement solutions, the consultant should be careful not to force her/him to do something s/he would regret later. The consultant should probe to make sure that the consultee is willing. If the teacher suggests what might be done, s/he is likely to be more committed to the procedure than if the consultant suggests it and the teacher "just agrees." In any event, the consultant should discuss any misgivings the teacher might have about a given procedure. This can be facilitated by the consultant showing the consultee s/he understands the costs involved.

Consultant: This would probably involve some work — distributing the materials and removing the cabinets for a game area.

(If the teacher has any reluctance, it is likely to arise here.)

Teacher: Well. That shouldn't be a problem. The cabinets will just have to be moved out of my room.

Consultant: And that shouldn't be a problem?

Teacher: I don't think so.

After arriving at a solution, the consultant should prompt the consultee to ask: "If I were successful in carrying out this solution, what would be the likely consequences?" This type of question often generates additional advantages and disadvantages of the solution.

Teacher:	I think that Jack and some of the others would study more but I'm not sure the Core teacher would go along with this.
Consultant:	OK. So maybe Core wouldn't be a good place to start implementing the program.
Teacher:	Well, Mrs. Hougler has a set way of doing things. I would rather keep it going when I am in the room.
Consultant:	You mentioned that some of the students are already doing their work so this program might not be necessary for everyone.
Teacher:	Yes, it doesn't seem reasonable to let them go to the game area when they are already doing the work. Besides, I don't have time to keep track of everyone.
Consultant:	I see. So maybe we should just use the program with those students who need some additional help.
Teacher:	Yes, but what do I say to the others?
Consultant:	Well, one thing that is usually helpful is to say that Jack or whoever is involved is trying to complete more work and that he needs special help to do so. Are there some alternate activities you could give the other students when they complete their work?
Teacher:	I think so.

Providing alternate activities for others helps to minimize the problem of singling out a child. Such procedures should reduce embarrassment and possible child-resistance to the program. The consultant must always be careful to discuss potential costs (e.g., more teacher effort and resources to implement the program) when specifying a new solution.

Notice also that the consultee makes the final determination for the proposed solution. This is imperative since the consultee implements the plan. If the consultant suggests a solution over the protests of the consultee, it will not likely be implemented.

Decide on Best Solution

When a probable solution has been decided on, the consultant should verify it by asking the consultee to paraphrase it.

Consultant: If we want Jack and some of the others to complete more work, what would be the best solution?

Teacher: Well, I think that if we set up a small game area in
the other corner of the room, the children could
use it when they complete their work.

It is important for the consultant to support a solution that can
be implemented "as is" or with a minimal amount of consultation or
training. Complex programs which require a great deal of consultee
time often fail because the costs of time and energy outweigh the
gains of student achievement or social development. It is also important that the consultee see immediate success and this may serve
as a potential reinforcer of his/her behavior.

Decide How the Planned Solution Will Be Implemented

Once a solution has been agreed upon, the next step is to decide
how the planned solution will be implemented and *who* will carry it
out. In general, it is advisable for the consultant and consultee to
collaborate on the overall design of the program while the consultee
takes major responsibility for the specifics in carrying out the program. Obviously, a teacher would have special skills in planning and
implementing a lesson. Thus, if the consultant suggested that the
teacher use some different questioning strategies to elicit more participation from the child, the teacher would likely be the one to decide on how the questions would be used to fit the content of the
lesson. Likewise, it is important to allow teachers or parents to use
their own skills in their own unique ways.

Because precision and consistency are essential to the success of
the consultation program, it is often helpful to prepare a written
plan or contract describing a detailed listing of procedures, setting,
conditions, resources (both personal and material) and the amount
of time the program will be in effect. The script or contract will
insure that both parties follow the agreed upon procedures and not
change their practices midway through the program. The plan also
reminds the consultee of the resources s/he needs to implement the
program. Still another advantage is that the plan or contract can be
incorporated into a final report as a description of the procedures
used to alter the client's behavior (Gelfand & Hartmann, 1975).

Table 6 presents a format that the consultant can use in writing
up the program. The consultant and consultee can discuss each
question sequentially, and if they wish to, they may add questions
such as, "How do the plans for phasing out the program provide
for generalization to other settings — home, neighborhood, etc.?"

Table 6: **Intervention Plan**

1. What are the client objectives?
2. What are the reinforcers for the client's desirable behavior? undesirable behavior? for the consultee's and consultant's desirable behavior?
3. What procedures will be used to decrease the undesirable behavior?
4. What procedures will be used to increase the desirable behavior?
5. Who will reinforce the client's desirable behavior?
6. What resources will the consultee need?
7. What methods will be used to prompt the client? consultee? Who will provide these?
8. Who will collect data?
9. Who will provide training, if needed, for the consultant?
10. When should the program begin and end?
11. Who should be notified of the program? Who should make the notification? When will the first meeting occur?

It is critical that the consultant and consultee work together to develop meaningful, reasonable and measurable objectives. The problem-solving approach assumes that if objectives are clearly specified with the consultee, the program will naturally move toward solving the problem. A good consultation objective contains the target behavior, specified conditions, and the time period and criterion level for the target behavior.

1. *What are the client objectives?*

The following transcript indicates how the consultant and consultee might specify an objective:

Consultant: All right, we talked about Jack's spending more time in his seat and completing more assignments.

Teacher: That's right.

Consultant: Good. Now we need to determine the number of assignments to be completed and how much of the time you would like him to be in his seat.

Teacher: Well, I would like him to complete all of his assignments.

Consultant: OK, I see that he is currently completing approximately thirty percent of his assignments. Do you think it's reasonable to expect him to complete all of his assignments immediately?

Teacher: Probably not, but that's what I'd like to see happen eventually.

Consultant: Right! But it may be too soon to expect that now. What would be reasonable to expect right now?

Teacher: Maybe completion of sixty percent of his assignments in language arts and social studies. But I would want him to complete more after awhile.

Consultant: I understand that and I agree with you. The reason for keeping the objectives lower now would be to allow him to experience success and then feel like working harder because he gets a payoff for it. If the goals are too high, students sometimes figure they can't do it and don't even try. So the goal of sixty percent completion in language arts and social studies sounds good.

Teacher: Yes, that would be a big improvement over the present situation.

It is important that goals be reasonable and achievable. This will help insure both client success and subsequent payoff for the consultee. It is also important to differentiate between long range goals and subordinate and performance objectives. In the preceding case, the goal is for the client to complete all assignments; yet, this may be too much to expect immediately. Consequently, subordinate and performance objectives are set in order to measure progress toward the ultimate goal. In stating the long range general goal, a time period for completion should be specified.

Consultant: So we are expecting him to complete sixty percent of his work by next week. When would you like him to be completing one hundred percent of his work?

Teacher: Maybe in three weeks.

Consultant: That means that after next week, he should be completing twenty percent more each of the next two weeks.

Teacher: Yes.

Consultant: These seem to be reasonable long range objectives for completion of work. How about accuracy?

Teacher: Well, he should get at least seventy percent of his answers correct. His accuracy level is satisfactory now; he just doesn't complete much of his work.

In order, then, to make sure that goals are understood by both consultee and consultant, the consultant restates the client objectives and writes them in the program plan. For example: "Jack will complete sixty percent of his language arts and social studies assignments with at least seventy percent accuracy the first week and complete an additional twenty percent with at least seventy percent accuracy each of the following two weeks."

2. *What are the reinforcers for the client's desirable and undesirable behavior?*

The treatment of most behavioral problems involves the administration of reinforcing events to the client. The consultant and consultee must be cautious in providing activities or awards which the child has identified as reinforcing rather than those the consultant and consultee presume are reinforcing. Since reinforcing events are, by definition, identified behaviorally rather than rationally, the consultant and consultee cannot conclusively select a reinforcer for a particular client without observing his behavior (Gelfand & Hartmann, 1975). While the consultant and consultee have discussed this already, it is still appropriate to verify it and write it down.

> Consultant: It seems like Jack was being reinforced by his friends for talking and being out of his seat on Tuesday, Thursday and Friday. On Monday and Wednesday your attention seemed to keep him on-task in the reading group.
>
> Teacher: That's right. We also said that he enjoyed playing games. I believe UNO is his favorite.

The consultant enters this in the script: "Children's attention reinforces off-task behavior on Tuesday, Thursday and Friday while teacher's attention reinforces on-task behavior on Monday and Wednesday. Games such as UNO are potential reinforcers."

A successful consultation program should also specify potential benefits or reinforcers to the consultee (parent, teacher, other) and the consultant. For example, the teacher might gain time usually spent on discipline for instruction. Or, s/he might have more positive interactions with the child. Likewise, the consultant may also see potential reinforcers for him/herself (e.g., gratification of changing teacher and child behavior). A more detailed description of consultant and consultee reinforcers is given in Chapter Nine.

The following transcript illustrates how the consultant and consultee can identify potential reinforcers for their efforts.

Consultant: Let's make sure that the program is having some pay off for both of us. Can you see some benefits for yourself if we are able to reach the objective?

Teacher: Well, I think I would have more time to help other children rather than always using my time to tell Jack what he should be doing.

Consultant: Good. Can you think of some other benefits?

Teacher: Well, I don't know if this is what you mean, but I have a project I have to complete for a course I'm taking at the university. Maybe I could use this.

Consultant: Great! So you might be able to get a better grade.

Teacher: I hope so.

Consultant: If we can reach the objectives, with your permission, I could use this as a demonstration project.

Teacher: What do you mean?

Consultant: Well, I could bring other teachers into the classroom to watch you implementing the program. Would that be OK with you?

Teacher: Fine.

3. *What procedures will be used to decrease the undesirable behavior?*

Some behaviors occur in excess in either their frequency, intensity, duration or inappropriateness and consequently need to be reduced. Examples of such behaviors often include stealing, fighting, crying, name calling. In addition, some clients may make excessive use of appropriate behavior. That is, they know what to do and say in certain situations, but they do it so much that they are obnoxious to others (e.g., the person who is constantly asking for help in class).

After identifying the excessive behavior, the consultant must ask if the conditions following the excessive behavior are helping to maintain it. If so, it is necessary for the consultant to teach the consultee to ignore it (extinction). The result should be a decline in the frequency of maladaptive behavior over time unless the target response (fighting, calling others names, etc.) is reinforcing.

There are some additional questions which the consultant and consultee must address before considering extinction as a reduction procedure.

Consultant: If we want Jack to complete his assignments, we must find some way to decrease his talking out and leaving his seat. How about using an extinction procedure?

Teacher: What do you mean?

The consultant in this instance forgot to consider the entry level of the teacher. As a general rule, it is best to *avoid* using technical language (i.e., extinction) that consultees may not understand. This is quite incompatible with the collaboration mode of consultation where the consultant and consultee are seeking solutions. In this case, the consultant was fortunate because the consultee sought out the answer (i.e., "What do you mean?"). Many times the consultees may think they should know the meanings of technical terms and either pretend to know them or become resistive to implementing them.

Consultant: Does this seem like a behavior you could ignore?

Teacher: I think so. The only time it really bothers me is when there is a lot of laughter or loud talk which may annoy others.

Consultant: Does this occur often?

Teacher: No.

Consultant: When you ignore Jack's behavior, you may find that it increases for a short period of time.

Teacher: Why is that?

Consultant: Well, all of a sudden, you are taking away his only means of getting attention.

Teacher: I see.

Consultant: Do you think others in the class would likely imitate his behavior?

Teacher: Probably five students sitting around him.

Consultant: Maybe we could set up a point system where the five children receive one point each time Jack completes five assignments. These points could then be used to purchase time in the game area.

Unless the teacher, parent, or others can consistently ignore the client's undesirable behavior, a new reductive procedure should be considered. Such a procedure might include removal of the client from the reinforcing situation (e.g., classroom) or withdrawal of reinforcers from the client (e.g., points).

4.   *What procedures will be used to increase the desirable behavior?*

Behaviors which already occur in the client's repertoire, but are deficient, call for techniques that will strengthen them   Some examples of behaviors which may need to be strenghthened are: attending to the lesson, completing assignments or interacting with others.

In order to strengthen behavior which is already in the client's repertoire, reinforcers in the natural environment (e.g., attention, approval and praise) should be used initially. These reinforcers are easy to deliver, and behaviors which are under the control of the natural environment are more likely to generalize or maintain. In instances where praise or approval is not capable of controlling the individual's behavior, however, activity or material reinforcers can be used. Material or activity (e.g., games) reinforcers may be necessary for some children for whom social reinforcers have little potency.

Consultant: The problem seems to occur during language arts and social studies. Let's just focus on that period. You said that you initially wanted Jack to complete sixty percent of his assignments with at least seventy percent accuracy and we agreed that Jack and these other boys who have trouble completing their assignments could earn time to play games in a designated area.

Teacher: That's right.

Consultant: If Jack completes an assignment with seventy percent accuracy, how many points should that assignment be worth?

Teacher: Well, I haven't thought about that. I'm not sure.

Consultant: I guess it depends on how fast the boys normally complete an assignment and how long you want them to play in the game area.

Teacher: Well, they should complete three or four assignments a day. I guess they could play in the game area for twenty minutes — no longer.

Consultant: How about if each assignment is worth one point and each point is worth five minutes in the game area?

Teacher: Fine. When would they receive these points?

Consultant: They should receive them immediately after they have completed an assignment.

Teacher: Well, I usually have reading groups so I can't check papers as soon as they're turned in.

Consultant: Do you allow any time to check individual work?

Teacher: There is generally five minutes between the groups when I check work.

Consultant: Suppose you allowed ten minutes between groups?

Teacher: I guess I could do that.

Consultant: That way each child can get points immediately if his work is completed. What shall we write on the plan?

Teacher: Well, each child will get one point for each successfully completed assignment. Each point is worth five minutes. Assignments will be checked between reading groups.

When the consultant asks the teacher to restate the procedures to be used, it helps to insure greater understanding and commitment from the consultee. A consultee may initially agree with an intervention program but when the details of how the program is to be implemented are discussed she may object to part of it. For example, a teacher may agree to use a game to reinforce a child's study behavior but only after school, not during school time. Thus, summary statements for the program plan allow for consultee objections.

Teacher: What can I use for points?

Consultant: I'll tell you about Mrs. Jones' system. Each child has a point card like a credit card. Each hole in the card represents one point, and points or punches are redeemable for time in the game area.

```
┌─────────────────────────────────┐
│  O  O  O  O  O  O  O  O  O      │
│  O       Jim's Credit Card    O │
│  O                            O │
│  O       Date . . . . . . . . O │
│   O  O  O  O  O  O  O  O  O     │
└─────────────────────────────────┘
```

Consultant: When would be a good time for each child to be in the game area?

Teacher: Well, any time between 9:30 and 10:30 a.m.

Consultant: Maybe you could make out a schedule and let each child sign up when he wants to use the game area.

5. *Who will reinforce the client's desirable behavior?*

Once a list of reinforcing activities has been completed, the next step is to determine who will dispense these. This should be someone who spends time with the client and who is valued by the client.

For example, playing a game of Monopoly is a reinforcing activity for some children, but this is often contingent upon the persons with whom they are playing.

The important point here is that many reinforcing activities are interpersonal, and some reinforcers require a particular individual to successfully deliver the reinforcer (Tharp & Wetzel, 1969). There are only two criteria for a reinforcing individual: (1) delivering high ranked reinforcers for the desired behaviors and, (2) dispensing these reinforcers on contingency. For example, if a child chooses staying up thirty minutes later each night to watch TV as a reinforcer, the parent would be an appropriate dispenser of that reinforcer. Or, a boy who wishes to play basketball after school may need the coach to provide this activity. In some cases where teachers are unwilling or too busy to dispense reinforcers, the consultant must identify someone (e.g., teacher's aide) who will monitor the client's behavior and dispense a reinforcer on contingency. In the case in point, the teacher is the appropriate individual to dispense the points.

Consultant: Is there anyone else who might deliver points right now?

Teacher: I can't think of anyone.

Consultant: Later on, if the system is working, we might ask some of the other children in the class to give out points.

Teacher: I think there are some children who would be capable of that.

6. *What resources will the consultee need to implement the program?*

It is critical that all materials be listed and acquired before the program is implemented. For example, if training for the consultee is necessary (see Chapter Eight), then handouts, books, audio or videotapes and equipment should be secured. If video or audio equipment is being used, it is critical to make sure the equipment is working and that backup equipment is readily available. In some cases special observation sheets must be designed. For the teacher or parent, contracts, tokens and lesson plans should be available.

If reinforcers are being used, they should be located so that they are out of the child's reach but within vision. Otherwise, the child may attend to the reinforcers rather than to the task at hand. One way to keep the reinforcement separate is to devise a "task" area and a "reinforcement" area (e.g., game area). These two areas should be separated if possible, perhaps by using separate tables, desks or rooms. Separating the two areas keeps the noise level down and helps the student and teacher to monitor the time spent in each area.

Consultant: What materials do we need for the game area?

Teacher: Well, we listed Clue, Life, Monopoly, UNO and Careers. I might talk to the librarian about getting some other games.

Consultant: We said that you could move your cabinet out of the classroom. We also need something to separate that area. Suppose you used your two bookshelves to separate it from the rest of the class? I think I could get a small rug to put in the back of the room. Can you think of anything else we need?

Teacher: What about schedules and credit cards?

Consultant: Right. I can help you make up some credit cards. Do you have a timer to control the amount of time each child is in the area?

Teacher: Yes, I have one at home.

Consultant: OK. Let's make a list: timer, schedules, credit cards, games, rug.

7. *What methods will be used to prompt the client and consultee? Who will provide these?*

If the client never or rarely emits the desired behavior and if you attribute this low rate to a deficient repertoire rather than to inadequate incentives, then the consultee should use prompts to start the behavior. The most common kind of prompt is instructions, but instructions, either written or verbal, are only effective when there are positive consequences for compliance. In other words, a good way to train a child to disobey is to issue numerous commands but not reinforce the child for obeying them. Instructions are also likely to prove most effective if they are carefully phrased. Suggestions made to young children should be unambiguous, consistent and intelligible, and it is advisable to use very specific terms. For example, rather than telling a child to "work hard," it would be better to say, "If you complete two assignments in the next hour, you can go to the game area for ten minutes." Or, you might say, "If you take out the trash and make your bed, you may stay up an extra half-hour tonight." This is both precise and stated in a positive manner. Instructions such as, "Clean up your room," sound harsh as opposed to, "As soon as you clean up your room, we can go skating." Precisely stated positive instructions with positive consequences attached are more likely to be followed.

Consultant: Let's list instructions so each child will know what is expected.

(Here it is a good idea for the consultee to state the instructions so that she continues to show ownership of the program.)

Teacher: Well, first, as we said before, for each assignment completed, each child will receive one point.

Consultant: OK. What else might you say?

Teacher: I could remind them to keep working.

Consultant: What about the game area?

Teacher: If they don't leave, I should remind them that the time is up and then start the next activity.

Consultant: Fine. Also, I can give you a signal by raising my right hand if you get busy and forget to award points or prompt the children when necessary.

8. *Who will collect data?*

Often before the recommendations can be accepted or rejected by the consultee, the responsibilities for monitoring the program must be considered. What are the individual responsibilities for collecting and analyzing the data? The consultee is generally the most appropriate one to collect assignments or record data when the consultant is not present. However, this usually depends upon the situation.

Consultant: We should try to gather some information to see if our program is working. If you could keep a record of how many assignments each child completes on a daily basis, it will tell us how the program is going. Since each child will be at his seat between 9:00 and 9:30 a.m., I will come in and observe their behavior next week. This way we can tell how much they are working and what, if anything, is keeping them off-task.

In some cases when neither consultant nor consultee is available, an aide or parent might be trained to observe the behavior.

9. *Is training of the consultee necessary?*

Many consultees will require assistance from the consultant in finding out how to go about implementing recommendations. This is often an essential part of the consultant's contribution and is another reason why the written recommendations should be discussed with the consultee.

There are a number of ways the consultant can determine whether the consultee needs training. First, the consultant might ask the consultee to role-play to decide whether she has the necessary skills to modify the client's behavior. Or, the consultant might observe the consultee during treatment to insure that treatment is being properly implemented. If the consultee needs additional skills, the consultant might provide written materials and/or audio or videotapes which model desired behaviors. Furthermore, the consultant might demonstrate the necessary skills for the consultee and then ask her to rehearse these until they are mastered. (Training will be discussed in detail in Chapter Eight.)

Consultant: Do you need any help from me in implementing the program?

Teacher: I don't think so. I hope I can remember to stop the reading group on time and check their papers.

Consultant: Maybe I could signal you with my right hand if you forget. We also need to set up times for the children to enter and leave the area.

10. *When will the program begin and end?*

The times a program should begin and end can also have a considerable bearing on the success of a program. A time should be selected when the client is neither fatigued nor eager to go to recess or somewhere else. If a program includes food reinforcers, it is important to conduct sessions at times when the client is at least moderately hungry, certainly not immediately after mealtime.

Timing should minimize inconvenience to the consultee. That means that the program should not be implemented at home during the family's favorite television show or when a teacher has a special class activity. If possible, the consultant should select a time when the consultee can discuss the problem without being under pressure to get back to her class or to take care of some similar duty. Starting a program the day before a vacation or on a Friday afternoon will likely end in disaster.

Consultant: We agreed to implement the program between 9:00 and 10:30 a.m. Right?

Teacher: Yes.

Consultant: Is this the best time?

Teacher: Yes, if we are going to start it during language arts.

Consultant: If you feel the program is interfering with some other activities, we can discuss it. Maybe we should set a time to discuss the program this Wednesday. Then if anything isn't going right, we can adjust it.

11. *Who should be notified of the program?*

Anytime a change program is being implemented, the child's parents should be informed. While parents may not possess the skills to design an intervention program for the child, they have the right to veto the program if they disagree with it and certainly should be encouraged to participate in it if they are favorable toward it.

Similarly, if possible, the child should be informed of the intervention program and be allowed to give consent or disagreement. Obviously, a child who is extremely young, autistic or retarded may not be able to make treatment decisions so these would be made by parents or guardians.

* * * * *

CONSULTING SKILLS INVENTORY

Directions: After each item check YES or NO to indicate whether the skill has been demonstrated.

DESIGNING THE INTERVENTION	YES	NO
1. Review information	. . . . .	. . . . .
2. Design a plan	. . . . .	. . . . .
3. Generate alternative solutions	. . . . .	. . . . .
4. Evaluate each solution	. . . . .	. . . . .
5. Decide on best solution	. . . . .	. . . . .
6. Decide how the planned solution will be implemented	. . . . .	. . . . .

* * * * *

CRITERION TEST

Directions: For the following situation write brief descriptions for each of the five steps in problem-solving.

Mrs. Moss requests your help with Jim because he fights excessively. In fact, he now averages one fight a day at school, and the kids in his classroom refer to him as "Bully Jim." Mrs. Moss says she's concerned about Jim's bullying other children but she's also concerned about Jim. He seems unhappy and has very few positive interactions with peers.

1. *Identify the problem:* ....
....
....
....
....
....
....
....
....
....

2. *Generate alternative solutions:* ....
....
....
....
....
....
....
....
....
....

3. *Evaluate the solutions:* ....
....
....
....
....
....
....
....
....
....

4. *Select the "best" solution:* ....
....
....
....
....
....
....
....
....
....

5. *Decide how the planned solution will be implemented:* ....
....
....
....
....
....
....
....
....

Suggested answers:

1.   *Identify the problem:* The problem seems to be that Jim fights a great deal and also that he seems unhappy. The desired behaviors are reduced fighting and more positive interactions with peers.

2. & 3.   *Generate alternative solutions and evaluate solutions:* (These steps are grouped together.) Alternatives should be generated both by the consultant and consultee.

    (a)   Punish Jim when he fights. (This may temporarily reduce fighting at school because the child becomes more fearful but may result in greater hostility than he previously had.)

    (b)   Contract with him and reward him for time periods when he does not fight. (This may work if the rewards are more potent than his current pay off from fighting. Otherwise, fighting will continue to be more attractive.)

    (c)   Contract with the class and reward the class when Jim does not fight. (This will involve the whole class with Jim's behavior and cause all the children to discourage fighting and encourage positive interaction.)

    (d)   Have a conference with Jim's parents. (This may be very beneficial in understanding Jim and in getting the parents involved in changing Jim's behavior. However, it is likely only a partial solution and better used in conjunction with another alternative.)

    (e)   Recommend therapy for Jim with the goal of improving his self-concept.

4.   *Select the best alternative:* The best alternative is simply the one which both the consultee and consultant perceive as most helpful and least time-consuming. In this case, they might choose (c) and (d). The advantages of using a contract in this case are: The teacher will be spending less time attending to Jim's fighting and the students will hopefully be discouraging Jim from fighting. The disadvantage for the teacher seems minimal. She must "write up" the contract with the students and discuss it with them. She must also purchase and deliver the rewards upon fulfillment of the contract.

5.   *Decide how the planned solution will be implemented. In designing the plan, the teacher should consider the following:*

    (a)   What are the client's objectives? The consultant, the teacher and Jim agreed that Jim would not fight for the next week. In addition, they might agree that Jim will have five positive interactions during science lab. A "positive interaction" is defined as any interaction between two or more people which excludes verbal or physical abuse.

(b) What are the reinforcers for the client's desirable and undesirable behavior? The reinforcers for Jim's fighting are encouraging remarks from children (e.g., "Come on, Jim, are you going to take that?"). Reinforcers from the class for positive interactions might include questions and positive comments. Reinforcers for the class might include field trips, a trip to the zoo, a trip to the museum, five minutes extra recess each day, class party, etc., depending upon their responses on the reinforcement completion blank.

(c) What procedures will be used to decrease undesirable behavior? The children should "ignore" Jim's verbal threats. However, if Jim hits someone, he will be removed from the classroom.

(d) What procedures will be used to increase the desirable behavior? The class will go on a trip on Friday afternoon if Jim has not been in any fights during the week. In addition, as a bonus if Jim engages in five positive interactions in science each day, he will be allowed fifteen minutes free time in the gym.

(e) Who will reinforce the client's desirable behavior? Children will reinforce positive interactions. The teacher will reinforce the class with a trip. The gym teacher will reinforce Jim with fifteen extra minutes in the gym.

(f) What resources will the teacher need? She will need a written contract, a written note to the gym teacher and permission to take a class trip.

(g) What methods will be used to prompt the client or consultee? Who will provide these? The teacher will prompt class members by saying, "Can you help Jim?" She might ask Jim, "Have you met your objective for the day?" The consultant will keep a record of the interactions to show the teacher. This may serve as both a reinforcer and a cue to provide additional prompts to the class or to Jim.

(h) Who will collect data? The consultant will keep a record of positive interactions and conditions which lead to them during science. Mrs. Moss, the teacher, will keep a record of fights.

(i) Is training of the consultee necessary? No.

(j) When will the program begin and end? The program will start Monday at 9:00 a.m. and end on Friday at noon.

(k) Who will be notified of the program? The child and his parents will be notified.

7

IMPLEMENTING THE INTERVENTION

Once the consultation program is designed, the next step is its implementation. Adequate implementation is dependent not only upon a good plan but upon mechanisms for monitoring and providing feedback to those consultees who are implementing the plan. Once these mechanisms have been developed, the consultant is ready to analyze why the consultee *is* or *is not* implementing the client program adequately.

In order to make this determination, the consultant should meet with the consultee periodically or on a daily basis. The degree of direct contact with the consultee in terms of program, design, implementation, and evaluation is based on two variables: (1) the agreement reached during the contract design stage and, (2) modifications of that agreement which may have been negotiated (Brokes, 1975). During this stage, the consultant and consultees should be aware that adjustments in time, resources, etc. may be necessary as the program evolves. These adjustments should be subsequently attached to the plan, either by an informal arrangement or by more formal procedures such as scheduled meetings to modify the plan (Kurpius & Brubaker, 1976).

Gather Observational Materials

In monitoring the implementation of the program, it may be helpful for the consultant to have predesigned observation forms. These forms can be used to monitor the consultee's behavior within specific time frames, to record data and provide feedback to the consultee. In addition, it is helpful if the consultant has a checklist for determining whether the consultee has the necessary resources. For example, if the consultee has not designed a pretest to measure client (child) readiness or backup reinforcers to motivate the client, the program may break down. This resource list should be completed before the program is implemented and the consultant should make sure that the consultant and consultee each have a copy of the program.

Table 7: **Resource Checklist**

Date . . . . Teacher . . . . Consultant . . . .

Circle YES or NO for each item.

1.	Pretest ready		YES	NO
2.	Teaching materials available			
	(a)	Printed materials - SRA handouts, word recognition cards, stories, etc.	YES	NO
	(b)	Packaged materials - Sullivan Reading Series, SRA, etc.	YES	NO
	(c)	Audio-visual material - filmstrips, etc.	YES	NO
	(d)	Timers, counters, etc.	YES	NO
3.	Reinforcers available			
	(a)	Food	YES	NO
	(b)	Tokens	YES	NO
	(c)	Activities	YES	NO
4.	Staff available			
	(a)	Teacher	YES	NO
	(b)	Aides	YES	NO
5.	Post-test ready		YES	NO

In addition to these materials, the consultant might keep a progress chart of consultee behavior. The chart might contain the percentage of appropriate consultee responses (intervention plan) and time line (days, weeks, etc.). These charts can be used to make others (principals, aides, supervisors, etc.) aware of the consultee's progress. It is important, however, that the consultee is aware that the consultant is keeping such charts and that s/he sees their value. Because the consultant needs to maintain the consultee's trust, a discussion of the use and value of charts and checklists should be held prior to the intervention and some agreement reached on which instruments to include.

Figure 17 provides an example of an observational form used to train staff trainees in the Behavior Analysis Project for the Follow-Through Program in Kansas (Jackson, Hazel & Saudargas, 1974). This form contains features essential to good observation forms: (1) the name of the client, the target behavior, beginning and ending times of observation; (2) teacher skills, frequency of appropriate and inappropriate occurences of the skills, and the time of each occurrence; (3) a summary of instructional criteria or objectives.

Table 8: Progress Chart – B.A. Specialist Certification*

TEACHING TEAMS

	K	1	2	3
Lead Teacher:				
Observation I				
Observation II				
Certification				
Aide:				
Observation I				
Observation II				
Certification				
Aide:				
Observation I				
Observation II				
Certification				
Aide:				
Observation I				
Observation II				
Certification				
Team Certified				

* Reprinted with permission of author and publisher from D. A. Jackson, M. M. Hazel and R. A. Saudargas. *A Guide to Staff Training.* Lawrence: University of Kansas Support & Development Center for Follow Through, 1974.

Figure 17. **Instructional Teaching Criteria***

Date . . . .   Teacher . . . . . .   Observer . . . .

I.   ON-TASK OBSERVATION

    Time began . . . .   Time ended . . . .   Total time . . . .
    Number of children in group . . . .
    Minutes: 1 . . .   2 . . .   3 . . .   4 . . .   5 . . . .
              6 . . .   7 . . .   8 . . .   9 . . .   10 . . . .
    Percent on-task = Number of children on-task   = ...
                     Number of children in group x 10 (min.)

II.   TEACHING OBSERVATION

    Time began . . . . .   Time ended . . . . .   Total time . . . . .

Contacts: 1 2 3 4 5 6 7 8 9 10 11 12 13 14 15 16 17 18 19 20 21 22 23 24 25 26 27 28 29 30

On-Task Contact

Off-Task Contact

Prompt

General Praise

Descriptive Praise

Token + Praise

Token Only

Disapproval

Accuracy

III. SUMMARY – INSTRUCTIONAL TEACHING CRITERIA

80% children on-task	Yes	No	0% disapprovals	Yes	No
100% on-task contacts	Yes	No	4 children in group		
100% contacts contain praise	Yes	No	working at 80%		
100% tokens paired with			accuracy	Yes	No
praise	Yes	No			
90% contacts with prompts			Timeout (if used)		
also contain descriptive			used appropriately	Yes	No
praise and tokens					

*   Reprinted with permission of author and publisher from D. A. Jackson, M. M. Hazel and R. A. Saudargas. *A Guide to Staff Training.* Lawrence: University of Kansas Support and Development Center for Follow Through, 1974.

By glancing at the observational form, the consultant and consultee can readily determine the relationship between the consultee
procedures and client behavior and whether objectives have been
successfully reached.

Monitoring Consultee Performance

Once all the observation forms and charts have been obtained,
the consultant is ready to monitor the program. The major purpose
for monitoring is to make sure the plan is being implemented according to design.

Plans often do not proceed according to specifications (see
Chapter Six) for one of four reasons. First, different instruments or
observation procedures are used to measure the problem behaviors
during the implementation phase than in the problem assessment
phase. For example, the consultant or consultee may change his/her
definition of the problem behavior (e.g., inititating a conversation)
from actually approaching someone and making a comment to interacting with someone (which does not require initiating a conversation). Or, the consultant may have used interval recording procedures to measure the frequency of problem behavior during baseline, but uses time-sampling recording procedures during the implementation of the program. In either case, the intervention plan cannot be evaluated because different measurement procedures were
used during the baseline and implementation phases of the program.

Secondly, consultees *may not be able* to implement the program according to specifications. This often occurs because consultees need further training. (See Chapter Eight.) Teachers and
parents often do not wish to admit they cannot properly implement
the program, and consultants often accept the word of the teacher
and parent without assessing consultee skills.

Thirdly, the complexity or the length of the program is often
so overwhelming that the program breaks down. In general, the
simpler the program, the more likely it will be properly implemented.
When intervention programs contain many components and are implemented over an extended period of time, the program often cannot be adequately monitored and breakdown will likely occur.

Finally, unforeseen problems may arise because of the effect
of the implementation plan on the system (e.g., school) or other
subsystems — grade levels, etc. (Brokes, 1975). For example, if the
teacher is using extinction procedures, the rate of target behavior
(e.g., negative comments) may increase at first. Unless the consultant and consultee have already discussed the temporary nature of
the problem, the teacher or parent may discontinue the program.

Giving Feedback and Reinforcement

In most intervention programs, the consultant gains immediate feedback and reinforcement through first-hand observation. That is, the consultant can see immediately whether the program is being implemented according to design, and if problems arise, they can be corrected immediately.

In addition, the consultant's or others' immediate observations can provide ongoing feedback to the teacher or parent while implementing the program. Teachers or parents can be cued for correct and incorrect implementation of the intervention. The cuing can be accomplished by means of prearranged hand signals, gestures or holding up cardboard signs (Gelfand & Hartmann, 1975). If this is too disruptive, the easiest way might be to interrupt the program and tell the consultee what to do. In some cases, a "bug-in-the-ear" device can be used. The consultee inserts a miniature earphone while the consultant can be seated as much as fifteen feet away with a wireless microphone. The consultant can give the teacher or parent instructions as s/he carries out the program with the child (Stumphauzer, 1971). A tape recorder amplifier helps transmit the instructions. The greatest advantage of this inexpensive equipment is that it helps to train consultees by (a) providing immediate suggestions and prompts to insure that the program is implemented properly, and (b) praising correct performance of the consultee immediately after its occurrence.

In observing and providing feedback at the same time, the consultant must be careful. If observation is continuous or the consultant is observing more than one problem behavior, the consultant will not likely have time to provide feedback to the consultee. If either of these problems arise, the consultant might alternate feedback and observation sessions, rather than try to conduct both simultaneously.

When it is impossible to make immediate observation, the consultant should try to contact the consultee by telephone. For example, the consultant might ask, "What did you say to get Bill to respond to the problem?" or "What did you say after Bill responded correctly?" When the teacher or parent gives specific examples the consultant will be more assured that the intervention plan is being implemented properly. The use of the telephone has an extra added advantage of saving time.

When direct observation is made, the consultant and consultee should arrange a short period after the observation for feedback. If this is not possible, the consultant can at least provide some casual feedback.

Consultant: How did you feel about the lesson today?

Teacher: I thought it went well.

Consultant: Mary, you did very well with Mike's math lesson. He seems to be doing more work than he was doing on Monday. You did a great job of giving him attention when he was working and ignoring him when he was looking around.

Teacher: Thanks. I didn't know whether I attended to him enough when he was working.

A brief interaction like this takes only a few minutes and can be done in the classroom following the lesson. Notice how the consultant first asked the consultee (teacher) how she felt about the lesson. If the teacher did not feel good about the lesson, it would be good for the consultant to first learn why the teacher is unhappy before giving feedback. Otherwise, the teacher may feel the consultant's feedback is inaccurate or possibly insincere.

In giving casual feedback, the consultant might want to make several more observations and then schedule a longer meeting to provide more detailed feedback and reinforcement. This should be done in a quiet place with few distractions. The consultant can begin the session by presenting the observation data to the consultee, reminding the consultee what s/he was looking for, and how it was recorded. It is generally useful if the consultant makes a copy of the observation sheet for the consultee.

Consultant: You can see on the form the number of times you attended to Jimmy when he was on-task and off-task. You can also see the number of times you used prompts, praise and disapproval. I computed an accuracy level for you. The second section shows the percentage of times you praised Jimmy correctly when he was attending to the lesson. How does this look to you?

Teacher: Well, it looks like I have been praising him more and his attending behavior has increased. There are several times that I have shown disapproval when I shouldn't have, though.

(At this point, if the consultee has no other concern, the consultant should praise those instances of positive consultee behavior.)

Consultant: You can see from the observation sheets that you praised Jimmy eighty percent of the time when he was attending to the lesson. Great! You can also see that when you praise Jimmy, he works harder.

Figure 18. Instructional Teaching Criteria Observation Form

Date: *3/27*   Teacher: *Barbara Stivers*

Observer: *C. Roberts*   Child: *Jimmy*

I.   ON-TASK OBSERVATION AND TEACHER OBSERVATION

Time began: *9:30*   Time ended: *10:00*   Total time: *30 mins.*

Child percentage of on-task behavior: 12/15 = 80%

Teacher percentage of desired behavior: 12/15 = 80%

CONTACTS

	1	2	3	4	5	6	7	8	9	10	11	12	13	14	15
On-task	x	x	x	x	x	x		x	x	x			x	x	x
Off-task							x				x	x			

TEACHER BEHAVIOR

Comments	1	2	3	4	5	6	7	8	9	10	11	12	13	14	15
Prompts		x													
General praise	x		x			x			x	x					x
Descriptive praise							x								
Token + praise			x	x									x		
Token only										x					
Disapproval							x				x	x			

II.   SUMMARY OF INSTRUCTIONAL TEACHING CRITERIA

80% child on-task behavior?   Yes√ No

90% teacher praise?   Yes   No√

0% teacher disapproval?   Yes   No√

(It is also helpful for the consultant to point out specific instances of desirable consultee behavior and in each instance to point out the positive effects the consultee's behavior had on the client.)

Consultant: I liked it particularly when you told him, "That's it" when he got the problem right. I think he was excited too. I made a note of that on the form and it looks like his attention was greater after that statement of approval.

Teacher: I was so enthused to see him stick with the problem rather than give up.

Consultant: I could certainly see your enthusiasm and I think he could too. He got a big smile on his face then.

When the consultee sees that specific behaviors are having a positive effect on Jimmy, s/he is also more likely to use these procedures in the future.

Once the consultant has discussed positive behaviors of the consultee, the next step is to tell the consultee what behaviors might be increased or used more frequently. Often a teacher or parent may be responding positively but just not doing it often enough.

Consultant: One thing you might do is make your praise statements a little more descriptive.

Teacher: What do you mean?

Consultant: Well, there was one time when you did this very well. You said, "Jimmy, I'm really happy that you remembered to go to the hundreds column and change a hundred to ten tens." Jimmy knew exactly why he was being praised.

Teacher: I guess I generally just tell him he is doing a good job.

Consultant: That's fine in many cases, but when you want to reinforce a specific response, it helps to tell him what he did and praise him for it.

Teacher: Maybe I could try that more in the future.

Consultant: Great! It probably would be good to think about specific responses you want to see during math.

When the positive consultee behaviors have been discussed, the consultant might mention any aspects of the program which the consultee is not implementing properly. The consultee will be more likely to discuss these at this juncture if they are brought up initially in the feedback sessions.

Consultant: One thing I noticed which you may not be aware of is that, even though you are not saying anything, when he turns around, you are staring and frowning at him.

Teacher: I guess I don't hide my feelings very well.

Consultant: That's hard to do. You may need to go one step further and look in the other direction. If you look at my notes on the observation form, even your nonverbal attention was enough to maintain his nonattending. This is not true for all children, however. The frown may be very effective in changing some children's behavior.

If the consultee has any questions about a technique, the consultant might demonstrate it through role playing. Otherwise, the consultant should provide a concluding summary or recommendation for the feedback session.

Consultant: My suggestion would be to give descriptive praise more often and to reduce the number of times you frown or give attention to Jimmy's nonattending. Keep up the good work!

Once desirable levels of the child's and consultee's behaviors have occurred for several days, the consultant can move from praising the consultee for each occurrence of desired behavior to an intermittent schedule of praise. Cossairt et al. (1973) found that teacher praise maintained when the teacher was placed on an intermittent schedule of praise by the consultant. This would seem to indicate that counselors and other supportive staff members' excuses that they do not have time for social praise of teacher behavior is invalid. By placing the consultee's behavior on an intermittent schedule of praise, the consultant can improve the consultee's behavior with a minimal amount of time.

Exercise: **Observation Form**

Directions: Given data on the observation form, answer the following questions.

1. What consultee behaviors should the consultant praise? . . . .
. . . .

2. What specific instances of consultee behavior should the consultant comment on? . . . .

3. What consultee behaviors should be used more frequently? . . . .
. . . .

4. What consultee behaviors should be used less frequently? . . . .
. . . .

Figure 19. **Instructional Teaching Criteria Observation Form**

Date: *9/1*   Parent: *Ms. Horsewood*

Child: *Bob*   Observer: *D. Stotler*

Target Behavior: Cooperation at home, viz., cleaning his room and taking out the garbage.

Desired Consultee Behavior: Give Bob a point and verbal reinforcement each time he cleans his room and takes out the garbage. (These chores are to be done daily.) Ms. Horsewood was instructed not to scold Bob if he did not exhibit the desired behavior.

Child Observation Sheet:

Behavior:	M	T	W	Th	F	S	S	M	T	W	Th	F	S	S
Cleaned his room	x	x	x	x	x	x	x		x	x	x	x	x	x
Took out the garbage		x			x		x		x	x	x			

Parent Behavior

	M	T	W	Th	F	S	S	M	T	W	Th	F	S	S
Gave points	x	x	x	x	x	x	x		x		x	x	x	x
Gave verbal reinforcement			x	x	x	x			x			x		
Scolding for not exhibiting desired behavior														

Criteria for Desired Change:

     Percentage of desired child behavior: 80% completion of both chores

     Percentage of desired parent behavior: 90% of time will give points and reinforcement; 0% scolding

Criteria Met?

Room cleaning?	Yes√	No	Giving verbal		
Taking out garbage?	Yes	No√	reinforcers?	Yes	No√
Giving points?	Yes	No√	Scolding?	Yes√	No

Suggested Answers:

1. Cleaning his room and taking out the garbage
2. None
3. Verbal reinforcement
4. None

Determine If There Is a Discrepancy in Consultee Performance

When the consultee is monitoring and there is a discrepancy between what the consultant *should* be doing and what s/he *is* doing, then the consultant should first ask, "Is the discrepancy due to a lack of skills?" For example, there are many discrepancies between what people say they will do and what they actually do. This may be due to low motivation or lack of interest or due to inadequate skills.

Determine If the Performance Is Due to a Skill Deficiency

How does the consultant know whether there is a skill deficiency which requires training? First, the consultant should determine whether the discrepancy exists just in the eyes of the consultant or if the consultee also knows that s/he is not doing what s/he should be doing. For example, when the consultant and consultee were designing the program, did the consultee know s/he should use descriptive praise? If so, did the consultant provide some examples and ask the consultee to provide some examples also? Did the consultant and consultee discuss when or under what conditions descriptive praise should be used? (See Chapter Six.)

Regardless of whether the skill was adequately identified or demonstrated, the consultant can often determine a skill deficiency by asking, "Has the consultee demonstrated the skill at any time throughout the program?" For example, in the aforementioned example, the consultee demonstrated the use of descriptive praise for a student's behavior. Thus, it is likely that the consultee knew how and when to use the skill but was not using it. In this case, the consultant praised him/her for using descriptive praise in the feedback session and discussed when the consultee might use the skill in future sessions. In addition, the consultee should attempt to praise each instance of this skill in future sessions, pointing out other instances when the consultee may have failed to use it. Observation can be useful here. For example, suppose the consultant enters the room the following Tuesday and uses the following graph to gather data.

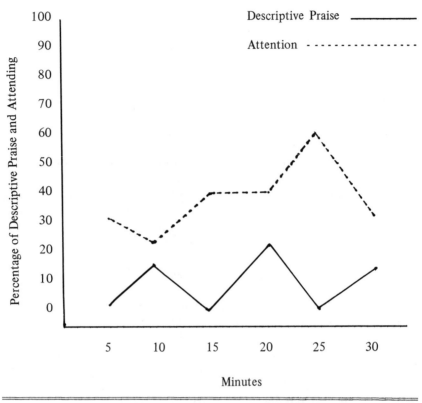

Figure 20: **Descriptive Praise and Attending Behavior**

If the consultant recorded this data on Tuesday and the consultee still failed to use descriptive praise, then the fact that the consultee failed to use the skill must be due to something other than a skill deficiency. When the consultee can demonstrate a skill but continues not to use it, then another procedure is needed in addition to training. It is likely in this case that the consultant must change the conditions under which the skill is demonstrated (Mager & Pipe, 1970), which usually means the consultant must change the consequences for the consultee's performance of the skill.

Jackson et al. (1974) cited four situations in which a consultee may *know how* to perform a skill but *does not* perform it. Answers to the following questions should be helpful in determining why the consultee does not perform the skill:

A.   *Are there unfavorable consequences for the consultee's performance?* For example, when the teacher uses descriptive praise with Jimmy, s/he is taking time away from her/his favorite reading group. Then, the consultant must ask:

Are the consequences for using the skill less favorable to the consultee than if s/he didn't use it? Is it punishing for the consultee to use this skill? If the answers to these questions are "yes," the consultant should make some changes. In the preceding example, the consultant could arrange another time to implement the program so that the consultee would not miss his/her favorite reading group.

B. *Are there more favorable consequences if consultees do things their own way or if they do nothing, than if they use the suggested approach?* For example a parent may prefer to use punishment because it stops the behavior momentarily and it is easy to use. Do consultees get the desired results when they use their own procedures? What payoff does the consultee get for using his/her own procedure? In this situation, the consultant might try to give the parent an alternative procedure, e.g., time-out, which gets the same result and is just as easy to use.

C. *Is there a reinforcing consequence for the desired behavior?* For example, a teacher may not care to use a procedure or program because there is no recognition from other school personnel. Is there any satisfaction for implementing the procedure? Are there more reinforcing consequences for not implementing the procedure? The consultant in this case should encourage other school personnel to comment on the consultee's program. However, if they fail to do so or if the consultee is not reinforced by their praise and no other reinforcers are identified, the consultant should probably select a new consultee to work with the client. (See Chapter Nine.)

D. *Are there barriers blocking the consultee's performance?* For example, a teacher may wish to implement a new program but because of her husband's serious illness is unable to give extra time to the program. What barriers exist to prevent the consultee's implementation of the procedures? Are there conflicting demands on her time? In this case, the consultant might attempt to find a new consultee or wait until the personal crisis has been resolved before implementing the program. In cases where the barriers can be reduced (lack of time, resources, etc.) the consultant may be able to reduce them enough so that the consultee can perform the necessary skills.

In addition to the four situations identified by Jackson et al., a fifth and final reason for lack of results might occur when the consultee may be implementing the intervention plan according to design but it has no effect on the client's behavior. That is, the program does not seem to be alleviating the client's problem. Here the original plan may need to be revised. For example, the teacher may be ignoring inappropriate student remarks but the behavior does not decrease. Ignoring behavior may lose some of its effectiveness when the client is reinforcing him/herself (i.e., saying to him/herself, "That was pretty clever"). In this case the teacher might use "mild reprimands" (i.e., "John, stop talking and open your book to page 119"). While many interventions work for most clients, specific clients, such as in the above case, may require a different treatment.

Exercise: **Skill Performance**

Directions: Given the following situation, go through the preceding questions and examples (A thru D) and identify what is likely causing the difficulty and what you as the consultant could do to remedy the situation.

Mrs. Sifert agreed to design a phonics program for one of her students. However, she will not be able to do it until she is off bus duty after school.

. . . .
. . . .
. . . .
. . . .
. . . .
. . . .

Suggested Answer:

In this case, there appears to be an obstacle (bus duty) interfering with the teacher's implementation of the program. The consultant might assist the teacher in gathering some materials that have already been developed. If the teacher still resists these efforts, the consultant should review some other questions. Is there more payoff for not implementing the program? What is it? The consultant should attempt to establish an environment where consultees will receive support for their performances.

Modify Tasks in Program Design

As an answer to each of the preceding questions (A thru D), the consultant and consultee should modify one or more of the existing tasks in the program design. For example, in question D, the teacher is unable to develop outside materials (instructional materials, games, etc.) because of her husband's illness. External problems (e.g., accidents, illness, competing events) will often arise for either the consultant, consultee, or client and can get in the way of implementing the program. In any case, the specific tasks in the program design which are affected should be modified. In the above illustration one task for the teacher was to develop individualized instructional materials for reading comprehension. Since she will not have time to develop these materials, perhaps the teacher and consultant might decide to procure some materials already developed.

Consultant: I can understand why you don't have time to develop new reading materials. Maybe we can get some individualized reading materials somewhere else.

Teacher: Have you seen the Sullivan Reading Series?

Consultant: No.

Teacher: I think those materials would be appropriate. They are programmed and the children can work independently at their seats.

Consultant: They sound OK and making use of them would give you more time to spend with your husband.

Teacher: Yes. Do we have any money in the budget for these materials?

Consultant: I can check. If so, do you want to order them?

Teacher: Yes.

Developing New Tasks in the Program Design

Good planning involves developing alternative plans in case some options are not available. By developing alternative plans during the meeting, the consultant and consultee can both save time and insure that the program will begin on schedule. For example, there may be no money in the supply budget to order reading materials or to implement the materials may require special training. In this case, the consultant and consultee would be wise to consider alternatives.

Consultant: In case there is no money available, maybe we should consider some alternatives.

Teacher: You mean something we could do if we can't purchase these materials?

Consultant: Yes, or if the materials require any special training. Do you have any ideas?

Teacher: Well, the reading specialist who serves this school could probably tell us.

Consultant: When does she come?

Teacher: She will be here a week from Friday, but we are free to contact her at any time. I could phone her this afternoon.

Consultant: Great! I will check to see if there is money in the supply budget for the Sullivan Reading materials and you can call the reading specialist to see if these materials require any training. You also might ask her if she has any comparable materials.

Because precision is so essential to the success of the intervention plan, the consultant should be careful to write down any modifications or new tasks which the consultee agrees to. This is particularly true where changes are made. Otherwise, either or both parties may forget and continue with the old program. The success of any intervention program rests with the specificity and consistency with which the program is carried out.

Training the Client's Behavior in Another Setting

In a treatment situation, there is the possibility that the presence of the consultee (parent, teacher, other) determines the client's behavior. That is, the child may only make appropriate responses (social, academic, etc.) in the presence of the teacher or parent. In the example cited earlier, the child may only complete his/her reading lesson for the teacher. Or, the presence of the consultant may serve as a cue for the teacher to implement the program when s/he may not do it otherwise. Since it is impossible for the consultant to be with the consultee or the the consultee to be with the client all of the time, the consultant should take steps to see that the desirable behavior generalizes across situations/persons.

Consequently, when training occurs in other settings (home, neighborhood, etc.) with other consultees (e.g., mother, father, friend), the child's behavior comes under the control of different individuals who are more likely to be in his/her presence. In addition, training sessions should be conducted in a number of different settings, if possible. This will promote the transfer of treatment effects to natural environment settings and increase the probability of maintaining their effects following the termination of treatment.

When training for generalization, the consultant should vary the times s/he appears in the home or classroom. Next, the consultant and consultee should establish a criterion for generalization. For example, the consultant and consultee may agree that generalization has occurred when the child has completed the reading comprehension assignment with eighty percent accuracy on an intermittent reinforcement schedule for three consecutive sessions.

* * * * *

CONSULTING SKILLS INVENTORY

Directions: After each item, check YES or NO to indicate whether the skill has been demonstrated.

IMPLEMENTING THE INTERVENTION	YES	NO
1. Gather observational materials	.....	.....
2. Monitor consultee performance	.....	.....
3. Give feedback and reinforcement	.....	.....
4. Determine if there is a discrepancy in consultee performance	.....	.....
5. Determine if performance is due to a skill deficiency	.....	.....
6. Modify tasks in the program design	.....	.....
7. Develop new tasks in the program design	.....	.....
8. Train the client's behavior in another setting	.....	.....

* * * * *

CRITERION TEST

Directions: Given the following observational data form, indicate which (a) consultee behaviors the consultant should praise; (b) specific consultee behaviors the consultant should comment on; (c) consultee behaviors that should be used more frequently; (d) consultee behaviors that should be used less frequently.

(a) ....

(b) ....

(c) ....

(d) ....

Suggested answers:

(a) Instances where Mrs. Perkins praised Laura and gave her a point
(b) More prompts, i.e., "Remember our agreement" and less disapproval for not playing quietly
(c) Descriptive praise + points and prompts
(d) Disapproval

Figure 21. **Instructional Teaching Criteria Observation Form**

Date: *4/16*   Parent: *Mrs. Perkins*

Observer: *C. Dance*   Child: *Laura*

Target Behavior: Quiet playing before dinner

Comments: *Contacts*

	1	2	3	4	5	6	7	8	9	10	11	12
Quiet	x					x	x		x		x	x
Non-quiet		x	x	x	x			x		x		

Parent Behavior:

Comments:

		1	2	3	4	5	6	7	8	9	10	11	12
Not enough prompts (Remember our agreement)	Prompts				x				x				
	General praise + points						x	x		x	x		
	Descriptive praise + points	x										x	x
Too much disapproval	Disapproval		x	x		x							

Criterion for success: Was it met?

100% of time give one point for each contact when quiet   Yes No√

Child playing quietly 80% or more of the time   Yes No√

TRAINING THE CONSULTEE

Each time the consultant works with a teacher or parent, that teacher or parent will learn some techniques for working with children. In fact, this, in addition to a savings in time, is one of the benefits of consultation over individual counseling. This argument is not always a convincing one for teachers, however, especially when they want someone else to take the child and "fix him."

Consequently, one of the tasks of the consultant becomes that of pointing out the advantages of the teacher working directly with the child. Central among these advantages is the fact that the teacher spends a great deal of time with the child and consequently knows his/her behavior patterns, while the consultant would spend considerable time just in becoming familiar with the child's behavior. Secondly, the teacher has already established a relationship with the child, in many cases a very positive one, and has the advantage of the child's desiring his/ her approval. In contrast, if the consultant worked with the child individually, it would take some time just to establish a positive relationship. Still another advantage of the teacher working directly with the child is that the problem behavior which has precipitated the referral is generally exhibited in the classroom. In a one-to-one situation, the behavior may not be apparent at all and obviously would be more difficult to deal with.

It should be noted here that the consultant's approach or manner may affect the receptivity of the consultee. Where negative value judgments are made about the teacher's techniques, resistance is likely to occur. If on the other hand, the consultant recognizes the skills of the teacher and treats him/her as someone capable of dealing effectively with the client's problem behavior, the results are likely to be much more positive.

Even given that the teacher is receptive and that the consulting relationship is positive, there may be times when the consultee needs specific information on how to carry out an intervention.

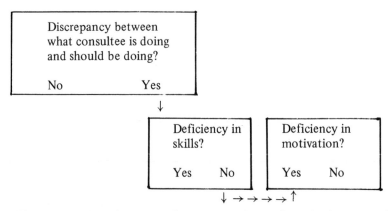

For example, the consultant may have found the consultee receptive, explained the program to him/her and still discovered a discrepancy between what the consultee is doing and what s/he should be doing. At this point, the consultant must determine the cause of the discrepancy, i.e., whether the teacher is not following the procedures because of low motivation, because of greater payoff for using conflicting procedures, or because s/he lacks the necessary skills and information to implement them. If the latter is the case, training is indicated. In order to make the training most effective, however, it is necessary to determine why the intervention did not work and just where the procedure broke down. This may require the consultant to spend some time in the classroom observing and perhaps recording on a checklist the presence or absence of teacher behaviors crucial to an effective change program. For instance, if the consultant's recommendations are to increase on-task behavior through reinforcement of the behavior each time it occurs, the following criteria may be important.

1. The child is contacted each time s/he is on-task.

2. Each contact contains praise.

3. Tokens, if used, are paired with praise.

4. Disapproval is not used.

5. Backup reinforcers for the tokens are prepared and ready.

6. Praise and tokens are given immediately after the desirable behavior occurs.

The consultant, while observing the classroom, could determine whether the teacher is in fact following these criteria, and if not, which procedures will require further training. If the teacher is doing all those things and the child is still off-task, the consultant can make a determination of what may be maintaining the off-task behavior in the absence of teacher reinforcement. In either case, this information is crucial to training the consultee.

Determine Training Needs

An important aspect of training is the assessment of exactly what the needs of the consultee are. If the consultant waits until s/he gets a referral, then the needs of the consultee are determined on the basis of the skills needed to implement the desired program. On the other hand, the consultant may find it more cost effective to predetermine the needs of consultees and perhaps offer training in groups rather than on a one-to-one basis.

Two basic approaches can be used to assess learning needs. These are the problem analysis method and the competency model method (Davis, 1974). Basically, the problem analysis method begins with a problem statement and is followed by a process to determine what learning needs are necessary to solve the problem. On the other hand, the competency model method requires, first, that a level of competence be determined after which learning needs for reaching this level are decided. These methods will be described in more detail below.

As Davis (1974) describes the problem analysis method, it involves seven steps: (1) stating the problem; (2) refining the problem statement; (3) supporting the problem statement; (4) finding the needs; (5) separating learning from non-learning needs; (6) putting needs in priority; and (4) testing commitment. First, the consultant must make sure that the consultee is stating the problem and not the solution. For instance, the teacher, when asked to state the problem, may say that Billy, a first grader, needs more motivation. When asked why, the teacher says, "Because he never pays any attention and he doesn't turn in his work."

The next stage is refinement of the problem statement. Probing in order to refine the problem helps clarify the *real* needs or concerns.

Consultee: Billy doesn't pay any attention or turn in his work.

Consultant: So Billy is not learning.

Consultee: Oh, I guess he's learning. His achievement test scores were very high.

Consultant: Then is he disturbing other students?

Consultee: No, he doesn't bother anyone.

Consultant: Then what is the problem with his not listening?

Consultee: Well, his mother is upset that he never brings home finished papers.

The third step is supporting the problem statement. As described in the chapter on assessment, frequency counts of specified behaviors can help determine the extent of the problem. In addition, group discussions or problem questionnaires such as that in Table 9 can help determine how many teachers/staff members consider specified behaviors as a problem and how adequate they feel in handling them.

Information from a checklist, such as the problem questionnaire, could provide the consultant with some guidelines for setting up group training to deal with difficult and frequent problem behaviors. In so doing, the consultant could save much time as compared to dealing with each of these consultees on a one-to-one basis.

Still another avenue for supporting needs is through past referrals. For instance, the consultant could go through records for the past two years or so and categorize the types of problems dealt with. At the same time, s/he could determine which problems were easily ameliorated and which areas the consultees had particular difficulties with or which required more extensive training. This could provide information concerning what should be stressed in future training.

The fourth step is to determine exactly what intervention is needed. Who needs to learn what? Is new information required? Will competing techniques be necessary? Does a decision have to be made? What resources are required?

After assessing specific needs, these must be separated into learning and nonlearning needs. If a decision needs to be made, this is a nonlearning need, while new techniques for handling inappropriate behavior may be classified as a learning need. The learning needs should then be prioritized and, finally, commitment to change must be assessed. If a teacher or parent is unwilling to come to training sessions or to try other methods, it makes no sense to provide training.

The second approach to needs assessment, the competency model method, begins with specifying what competencies are expected. These competencies would have to be stated in measurable terms. Then, assuming that a consultant had established the criteria for competency in a given area, e.g., child management, the next step would be to determine the discrepancy between actual performance level and the expected level. This could be done through simulations or from actual observation. An additional tool may be questionnaires on which personnel state whether they think they need additional help or training in a given area. Also, as in the problem analysis method, priorities need to be assigned and level of commitment determined before training begins.

Table 9: **Problem Questionnaire**

Name .... Date ....

Position ....

Rate the following behaviors in terms of their occurrence as well as the degree of difficulty you find in dealing with them. Use a 1 − 3 rating for each using the following key.

FREQUENCY and OCCURENCE   DIFFICULTY IN DEALING WITH IT

FREQUENCY and OCCURENCE	DIFFICULTY IN DEALING WITH IT
1. Does not occur	1. No difficulty
2. Occurs sometimes	2. Some difficulty
3. Occurs often	3. Much difficulty

Occurrence	Difficulty		
....	....	1.	Out of seat
....	....	2.	Talking out or interrupting
....	....	3.	Shyness
....	....	4.	Poor peer relationships
....	....	5.	Cheating
....	....	6.	Lying
....	....	7.	Stealing
....	....	8.	Failure to complete assignments
....	....	9.	Fighting
....	....	10.	Poor self image
....	....	11.	Other ....
....	....	12.	....
....	....	13.	....
....	....	14.	....

Provide Training

Training can take place in individual cases or it can be given on a group basis. While group training would be most efficient in general, there are instances where a consultee may be having particular difficulties which are not common to other persons in the institutions and/or which may require special procedures. In such cases, individual training seems warranted.

Individual Training

Specifically, before training is to occur, the consultant must determine which skills are missing. After observing in the classroom and recording the presence or absence of certain consultee behaviors crucial to the change program, the consultant can begin working on the behaviors which are lacking. For instance, Mrs. Cooney, the consultant, and Mrs. Tynan, the consultee, had worked out a change program to increase Tony's positive interactions with peers. The plan included the following consultee behaviors:

1. Each time the client initiated a positive interaction, he was to receive a token.

2. Tokens were to be paired with praise.

3. Tokens were to be used for "buying" various items from the reinforcement menu.

4. The teacher was to note each negative interaction and, at a specified period right after school, she would discuss these with Tony and teach him alternative positive ways to deal with the situation.

The consultant observed and noted the following:

(a) The teacher was inconsistent in giving tokens. If a class were in progress, Tony might not get a token for positive behavior.

(b) The teacher sometimes paired tokens with praise and did not at other times.

(c) The reinforcement menu contained only three items and on one occasion when it was time to trade tokens, Tony said he did not see anything he wanted to buy.

(d) After school, the teacher pointed out some negative interactions and asked Tony what he should have done. Tony responded, "Be nice." The teacher said, "OK, then. Try harder tomorrow."

When Mrs. Cooney, the consultant, looked over the data, she decided that the following skills needed some attention:

1. An operational definition of the problem behavior and desirable behavior should be made, and the consultee and consultant should agree on exactly what constitutes positive interactions and negative interactions. Since this was not clear in this case, it was not possible to determine whether the teacher's inconsistent use of tokens was due to her missing some positive behaviors or just defining positive behavior differently than the consultant.

2. The consultee needs practice in giving tokens for all positive behaviors, even when other activities are going on. This could be done through a role-playing situation where the teacher will teach a group and still watch for Tony's positive behaviors. The consultant could role-play Tony and let the teacher dispense tokens. This could be followed by a discussion of difficulties in observing both Tony and the rest of the group. If the consultee still had difficulty dispensing tokens consistently, the consultant might come to the classroom for awhile and give prompts. That is, if the teacher missed a positive interaction, the consultant might hold up a small card, etc. signaling the teacher that a token should be given.

3. In conjunction with giving tokens consistently, the teacher should practice giving praise as well. The consultant and consultee may generate various ways of giving praise without using the same words over and over. And if a class is in progress, the teacher may simply pair the token with an approving smile, a pat on the shoulder, etc.

4. Some work needs to done on constructing menus. The teacher's list is quite small and apparently does not include things that are reinforcing for Tony. They may first decide how to do an incentive analysis and then include many items which might be reinforcing to Tony. Otherwise, he will lose interest in working for tokens since there is nothing on the list he cares about earning.

5. The teacher needs to learn skills in teaching alternative positive behaviors. Since she was not confident about teaching Tony new behaviors, she allowed him to make a general statement such as, "Be nice." With training, she could learn new behaviors to teach him, then let him practice the new behaviors, reward him for exhibiting them in practice, and later reward him for exhibiting them in a real situation.

The consultant in this instance taught the alternative behaviors by first giving instructions or information about them, then modeling them, allowing the consultee to practice, and finally giving feedback on the consultee's performance. After providing training, the effects are likely to be more positive if the consultant continues to monitor the case for awhile. This may involve no more than asking the consultee if the client's behavior is changing and if not, to discuss factors which may be impeding progress.

Obviously, individual training is costly in terms of time. However, it has the advantage of being specifically geared for the consultee and consequently should be more effective in producing changes. Individual training in many cases will generalize also so the consultee will be taking skills learned in one particular situation and revising or gearing them for use in similar situations.

Group Training

Group training can be a very cost effective approach since it reaches several people with the cost of only one leader. There are obvious disadvantages, however. Because it is extremely difficult to get a homogeneous group to work with, some participants will be very familiar with material presented while others have no knowledge of it. Some problem areas dealt with may be common for some participants but not for others. In short, the training will likely be general in order to meet some of the needs of all the participants, but in the process, will not meet all the needs of any one person.

To cut down on this, some procedures can be employed to make the group more homogeneous. Perhaps consultees could be selected for group training on the basis of common problems. Or, as mentioned before, consultees who express on a checklist a need for certain information could be grouped together for training. In some cases, the consultee may wish to implement a program with a client in more than one environment. Here the consultant may wish to contact and train others (friends, employees, teachers, parents, etc.) as necessary. Various formats have been used for group instruction and these will be discussed separately.

Workshops:

Workshops usually involve participants for a consecutive period of several hours or several days. In these sessions, participants typically receive information through lectures, films, etc. but they are also involved in activities practicing what they are being taught. By having intensive instruction in a brief period of time, scheduling is easier. Also, more material can be covered since no time is spent in reviewing previously covered material.

One disadvantage of workshops (at least the ones held for a consecutive period of time) is that participants do not have any time between sessions to put into practice what they are learning, i.e., to try out their skills in an actual situation. This is why simulation is very important. Even though it is not a real-life situation, it can be made realistic and gives the consultee a chance to practice, get corrective feedback if the skill is not being implemented properly, and ask questions about areas which are not clear.

Unfortunately, even with workshops as long as two or three days, there is a limit to the depth of material which can be covered. It is possible to give a certain amount of information but difficult to teach participants how to do high level activities such as designing and implementing complete behavior change programs.

For workshops to be most effective, however, the leader/consultant should have objectives which are initially stated for the participants. Since workshops are often presented with the goals of teaching participants new skills or helping them to apply information, these goals should be specifically stated. And, to meet these, the workshop leader should present the necessary information for achieving the objectives and give opportunities for applying the information or practicing the newly learned skills. Without this, generalization to the "real" situation is likely to be poor, and in addition, the number of times that the skills are performed poorly or incorrectly is increased.

If a workshop is requested by a group of parents or teachers in a specific area, the next step is determining who will serve as the workshop leader. If the consultant has the skills to lead the group and the group feels comfortable with him/her, then s/he might be the most likely choice. However, if either of these conditions does not exist, the consultant or consultee might look elsewhere. Often the expertise for conducting successful in-service workshops can be found locally. It is suggested that internal resource persons who have the skills be identified and used where possible because participants often feel more comfortable and more free to participate when they are familiar with the leader.

Consultants should compile a list of potential workshop leaders on three by five inch cards. Each card should include:

1. Name of workshop leader
2. Address
3. Qualifications
4. Skill areas
5. Previous experience
6. Title or affiliation

In addition, the consultant may wish to make evaluative comments based on past performance. Workshop participants (consultees) can use these cards in reaching a proper decision on who will lead a particular workshop.

Mini-courses:

Another format for training consultees is through mini-courses. Mini-courses, as defined by Walter Borg (1972), are "individualized multi-media learning packages designed to help teachers develop instructional skills." As conceived by Borg, these courses can provide information, practice, and feedback on certain pre-specified skills. Weekly sessions may be held for five or six weeks, of course, depending on the number and complexity of the skills to be taught.

The following steps may be followed in setting up a mini-course:

1. Determine the objectives for the course (both cognitive and skill areas).

2. Develop a pretest keyed to the objectives and administer this at a pre-mini-course session.

3. Design instructional units for each skill or concept area to be covered. Instructional units may include: (a) either a film or other media presentation or perhaps a brief lecture presentation explaining the skill area, (b) model films showing application of the skill, and (c) time for practice or rehearsal with corrective feedback.

4. Since mini-course participants may have a diversity of experiences and training, the pretest can allow for individualized training. Because the pretest is keyed to the objectives and the various objectives will probably be covered in separate mini-courses, participants need not attend the mini-courses covering knowledge or skills they already possess.

5. Give post-tests to evaluate skill and knowledge acquisition.

Suppose, for example, that the consultant finds classroom management to be a common problem in a particular school. Mini-courses may be developed to teach the following skills:

1. Operationalizing the problem behavior
2. Observing the recording behavior
3. Identifying incentives
4. Increasing behavior
5. Decreasing behavior
6. Teaching new behaviors

A pretest could show the levels of proficiency at which the consultees are currently operating and help determine which mini-courses they should attend. In the mini-courses themselves, after information is presented, the consultees should be given written exercises in the skill areas and then be asked to do simulations, applying the knowledge they have gained. A criterion test at the end of each mini-course would point out which consultees might need additional training.

Borg et al. (1970) have identified four serious deficiencies in conventional in-service training programs:

1. The emphasis is on telling rather than on doing.

2. Instruction is general rather than specific.

3. Effective models are not provided.

4. Effective feedback is not provided.

Using the format described above, each of these weaknesses would be overcome. That is, doing would be emphasized, instructions would be specific, models would be shown, and feedback would be provided.

Seminars:

Related to the mini-course but perhaps of longer duration is the seminar. Because seminars often last for fifteen or sixteen weeks, there is ample opportunity for consultees to practice the skills they are learning and to discuss with others the problems they are having. In fact, the group discussions are often quite helpful. One parent may have special insight into a particular problem behavior as a result of dealing with it successfully, or one teacher may be able to give another teacher an idea or perhaps the encouragement needed to follow through on a plan.

Material can be presented in a seminar just as in a workshop or mini-course but there should be opportunities for practicing the skills learned. Evaluation may take place on a pre-post-test basis or may be done throughout the course by evaluating skills after they have been presented and participants have had an opportunity to practice and implement them. Because the seminars are extended over several weeks, it is possible to get more in-depth evaluations. That is, paper-pencil tests can be given to measure consultees' understanding of the principles presented, simulations can be used to measure applications of the principles, and real life cases can be used to measure actual generalization effects to the real situation, e.g., the consultee's ability to apply the principles in a real setting.

Problem-solving Case Approach:

Still another training approach is the case study or case conference. Here, the consultees may ask for help with a specific client, and the consultant works with people involved with that client. For example, if the client were a student, all the teachers involved with the student may be invited to participate in the case conference. If the client were a child referred by parents, the parents, perhaps a teacher, and/or significant others in the child's environment could be invited to participate. Or, if the client were a patient at a mental health center, any staff member involved in his/her treatment program may be invited to attend the conference.

The case conference or case study approach is designed to study one client's behavior, to determine some antecedents of the behavior, and to design a change program for him/her. In general, a problem-solving approach can be used. This could consist of the following:

1. *Define the problem behavior.* This consists of the consultee stating why s/he is referring the client and describing the problem behaviors that the client exhibits. After the consultee describes the problem behavior, anyone involved with the client will give information concerning his/her behavior.

2. *Identify desirable behavior.* The group then determines how the client "should" be behaving and states these behaviors specifically.

3. *Participants in the case conference state possible ways of getting the client to exhibit the desirable behavior.* Any alternative is acceptable at this time. That is, the initial step is to generate alternatives, and the evaluation can come later.

4. *Evaluate the alternatives.* Decide which of the suggestions seem most practical and most likely to have the greatest effect with the least cost. At this point, the consultant may become more active in training. For example, if the members suggest a particular change they would like to see but do not know how to effect it, the consultant may offer specific information at this time.

5. *Decide on the best alternative.*

6. *Decide how to implement the alternative.* Decide who will be involved in carrying out the plan, what resources will be needed, when it will start, and who will be responsible for each phase of the plan. It may well be that one person will not have to take on the whole change program since several people are concerned with the problem behavior and have been involved in working hard toward its amelioration.

Bibliographic Approach:

Necessary training in some cases may be readily taken care of through books designed specifically to teach various principles of behavior change. For instance, if a consultee's skill deficiency seemed to be in the area of identifying positive reinforcers, s/he may simply be given a handout or a book containing instruction in that area. Of course, for this approach to be effective, the consultant should have a follow-up session to determine if the consultee has in fact read the material and if s/he understands the concepts presented. Some examples of topics which may be included and which can be dealt with through written information are given below.

PARENT TRAINING IN CHILD MANAGEMENT:

Becker, W. C. *Parents are teachers: A child management program.* Champaign, IL: Research Press, 1971.

Krumboltz, J. D. & Krumboltz, H. B. *Changing children's behavior.* Englewood Cliffs, NJ: Prentice Hall, Inc., 1972.

Patterson, G. R. & Gullion, M. E. *Living with children: New methods for parents and teachers (2nd Ed.).* Champaign, IL: Research Press, 1976.

Sloane, H. N. *Five practical behavior guides.* Fountain Valley, CA: Telesis Limited, 1976.

TEACHER TRAINING IN CLASSROOM MANAGEMENT:

Becker, W. C., Engleman, S. & Thomas, D. R. *Teaching a course in applied psychology.* Chicago, IL: Science Research Associates, 1971.

Harris, M. B. *Classroom uses of behavior modification.* Columbus, OH: Merrill Publishing Co., 1972.

Krumboltz, J.D. & Krumboltz, H.B. *Changing children's behavior.* Englewood Cliffs, NJ: Prentice Hall, Inc., 1972.

Meacham, M. L. & Weisen, A. E. *Changing classroom behavior: A manual for precision teaching.* Scranton, PA: International Textbook Co., 1969.

Swift, M. S. & Spivack, G. *Alternative teaching strategies.* Champaign, IL: Research Press, 1975.

TRAINING IN CONTINGENCY CONTRACTING:

DeRisi, J. W. & Butz, G. *Writing behavioral contracts: A case simulation practice manual.* Champaign, IL: Research Press, 1975

Homme, Lloyd, et al. *How to use contingency contracting in the classroom.* Champaign, IL: Research Press, 1969.

TRAINING IN THE USE OF TOKENS AND IDENTIFYING REINFORCERS:

Alvord, J. R. *Home token economy: An incentive program for children and their parents.* Champaign, IL: Research Press, 1973.

Rogers, J., Geis, G. L. & Pascal, C. E. *Rewards in the classroom: The consequences of learning.* Montreal, Canada: G/P Associates, 1974.

Group and Individualized Training

Perhaps the greatest benefits in training programs come from large group presentations combined with a built-in individualized component. Since certain information is generally useful or necessary across a whole group, the large group presentation would be the most efficient way to present this information. Yet, the greatest effect from a program is realized when consultees are able to to discuss the specific problems they are having and look for help in applying behavior change principles to these specific problems. Consequently, the first part of each group session may be given as a large group presentation and then be followed by small group work where each group member can apply the information to his/her own specific "clients." Below is an example of a training program combining both the group and individualized approach.

Training Program Combining Group and Individual Approaches

Several parents of children coming to the mental health center indicated that they had difficulty getting their children to "mind." In other words, the children were very defiant and either openly refused to comply with parental requests or ignored them. Ten of the parents involved indicated that they would be interested in a parent education program designed to last seven weeks. The general format and plans for the sessions follow.

Session One: Getting Acquainted and Operationalizing Behavior

Objectives:

1. Parents will be able to tell other members about themselves and their children.

2. Parents will be able to operationalize behavior.

One of the tasks of Session One was to make the parents comfortable and help them get to know each other. Introductions were made initially, and parents gave a brief explanation of why they were attending the workshop. Then parents were asked to complete a bipolar adjective checklist describing the behavior of the child with whom they were having the most difficulty and also to respond to a brief test covering some of the cognitive concepts to be presented during the seven weeks. Following this, the leaders showed a twenty minute film demonstrating how children learn to behave badly.

The last hour of the session was geared to teaching the participants how to operationalize behavior. To make it more applicable to each individual, each person wrote five behaviors which s/he disliked in his/her child and then gave operational definitions of each. These were discussed in small groups, with a leader and other small group members giving corrective feedback. As homework for the week parents were asked to observe incidents of undesirable behavior and write these down. Any behavior not operationalized was changed to an operational definition.

Session Two: **Observing and Recording Behavior**

Objectives:

1. Given a role-playing situation, participants will be able to observe the frequency of pre-specified behaviors.

2. Given a recording sheet and graph paper, participants will be able to graph the frequency of pre-specified behaviors.

This session began with a brief review of the previous session and a few examples of parents operationalizing behaviors they had observed. Then two leaders role-played a ten-minute parent-child interaction and the participants were asked to observe and tally the frequency of parent requests and child noncompliance. This interaction was audio taped so that it could be used again when participants checked their tallies. Participants were then taught to graph the data. Following this, they broke up into small groups again (two or three people) and talked about specific problems they had observed the week before. They got additional instruction from the small group leader on how to observe and record the problem behaviors they were experiencing. Members decided which problem behaviors they wanted to deal with initially and were instructed to observe these the following week.

Session Three: **Increasing Behavior**

Objectives:

1. Participants will be able to identify reinforcers for their children.

2. Participants will be able to write reinforcement menus.

3. Participants will be able to give verbal reinforcement on contingency.

Session Three began with the leader showing parents ways to determine what is reinforcing for their children. In addition to the activities and items parents already knew about, the leader showed forms, observation techniques, etc. which could be helpful in identifying additional reinforcers. The leader then showed sample reinforcement menus and discussed how to establish cost for the various items. Finally, there was a discussion on giving reinforcement immediately and on contingency, and the leader showed the group a tape which modeled this skill.

Participants then broke into their small groups and went over their observational data for the previous week. Leaders helped determine problem areas and gave suggestions for ameliorating the "snags." Participants role-played with each other, first finding reinforcers for their children, then showing their children a sample reinforcement menu and explaining its use. Members gave feedback to each other on how they performed this task. The leader role-played a child and parents took turns role-playing the parent. Their goal was to reinforce pre-specified behaviors immediately and on contingency. At the end of the session, the group leader showed several parent-child interactions on videotape, and each participant wrote on his/her answer sheet the time when reinforcement should have occurred and also wrote a sample verbal reinforcer. This response gave the leader an opportunity to evaluate particpants' abilities to implement what they had learned that session.

Session Four: **Decreasing Behavior**

Objectives:

1. Participants will be able to list at least four ways for decreasing behavior.

2. Given some descriptions of situations, participants will be able to tell which techniques are best for decreasing behavior and give a rationale for their choices.

Session Four began with a presentation of ways to decrease behavior, namely extinction, time-out, response cost and punishment. The presentation also included information on when to use each of these techniques, how to implement them, etc. This was followed by videotaped segments in which the problem behavior was manifested by a child and then was decreased. The leader stopped the tape after the behavior was shown and the group discussed which technique to use.

In the small groups, parents discussed their success in increasing a behavior during the previous week. They made lists of behaviors they would like to decrease and together determined which techniques to use to decrease them. The session ended with members stating what behaviors they would work on decreasing during the upcoming week.

Session Five: **Contracting**

Objectives:

1. Parents will be able to write behavioral contracts.

2. Given parent-child conflicts, parents will be able to negotiate and write contracts to solve the problems.

Session Five began with the leader describing the advantages of contracts, then explaining the basic components of a behavioral contract, and giving various samples of these. The leader also described conflict situations and asked parents to write behavioral contracts. Suggested answers were given so that the participants could compare their answers with these. After breaking up into small groups, parents went over their homework. They then used some behaviors they had listed earlier (behaviors to be increased and decreased) and wrote sample contracts for these After discussing the completeness of the contracts, parents role-played negotiating the contracts with their children.

Session Six: **Summing Up**

There was no large group presentation at this session. All participants met with their small group leaders and spent the first part of the session going over their problems and progress. Then the leaders gave the parents two hypothetical situations and asked them how they would deal with these. Discussions followed, with the next few minutes devoted to additional problems they wanted to talk about. The session closed with parents filling out the behavior checklists and taking the test on concepts presented in the workshop.

Session Seven: **Follow Up**

This session was held one month after the end of the last session. The purpose was to help maintain the positive change approaches parents had initially instituted. Also, this period of time allowed parents to see how the program was functioning and to note difficulties which arose. Leaders helped trouble shoot problems at this time and gave a great deal of positive reinforcement to parents for techniques they had tried.

The workshop described above actually took much leader time because of the individualized component. Yet, the effectiveness was great because the individual attention and reinforcement for implementing the techniques created much involvement on the part of parents and consequently more behavior change in the children.

Attend to Training Tips

No matter which format the consultant chooses for training, there are certain factors which must be taken into consideration for maximal effectiveness.

1. *State objectives clearly.* One of the skills often taught in workshops is how to write good objectives, since one must know where s/he is going in order to know when s/he has reached his/her destination. This is equally true for the workshop leader. Let the participants know what they should be able to do following the workshop or individual sessions.

2. *Give information necessary for participants to be able to perform the desired skills.* Whatever format is chosen for presenting information (lecture, books, films, audio or video tapes), it should be given clearly and concisely. It should also be complete enough so that participants have the knowledge necessary to perform the desired skills.

3. *Give practice in applying knowledge, i.e., get the learner involved.* One big criticism of many workshops is that they simply dispense information. While there is merit in this, the crucial factor is whether or not participants are able to apply that information. By asking participants to apply the information, it is possible to determine the real effect of the instruction. It should be noted that in addition to giving instructions, it is often helpful for the leader to model the application of information presented.

This way, the leader·tells participants how to do it, shows them how to do it, and then instructs them to try it on their own. If the instructions and model have been adequate, the participants should perform at least well enough to achieve some degree of success.

Some practice situations will have to be simulated. For instance, if the objective is to teach consultees how to individualize instruction, the leader may first present information on various ways to individualize, giving necessary instructions for doing each, and then giving examples of how a teacher with a particular group of students implemented the individualization program. The model may vary from observing an actual classroom situation to filmed excerpts from classroom activities to displays of materials (learning centers, individualized learning packages, etc.) used to individualize instruction. After showing the model, the consultant may give a hypothetical list and description of students and ask the consultees to design instructional units for the students. Or, in this case, the consultee may use his or her own group of students and design individualized instructional programs for them. In any case, the learner gets involved, not only in seeing how to do something, but by actually *doing* it.

4.   *Give feedback on performance.* The best feedback system is a two-way one, with the consultant giving feedback to the consultee on his/her performance but also with the consultee giving feedback concerning problem areas s/he's experiencing. The mutual feedback helps make the consultant aware of how effective the training is because it can be judged both from his/her perspective of how well the consultee is performing after training and from the consultee's perceptions of how clear the instruction has been. Feedback should be given frequently to allow the consultant to change procedures which are ineffective and for the consultee to correct errors in procedures or techniques.

5.   *Use the feedback to make productive changes.* Through the use of frequent feedback, the consultant can keep abreast of changes that need to be made in training and can adjust accordingly. For instance, if consultees have had instruction on behavior shaping and still seem unable to implement it, information in this area should be presented again, with opportunities for supervised practice.

And, perhaps the information should be presented differently. If the original format or procedures were ineffective, i.e., not accomplishing the objectives, alternatives should be sought. On the other hand, if consultees seem ready to move on to another topic, the consultant should be flexible enough to do so.

6. *Help consultees establish programs which will be rewarding.* Behavior which is not rewarded will not be maintained, so the training of consultees to do something for which there is no payoff is futile. In contrast, if the consultee practices skills that result in better behavior by the child, the consultee is likely to repeat these skills. An ideal situation is to choose a behavior which is bothersome to the consultee but which can be modified easily. Thus, there is quick payoff for the consultee. If the selected problem is *very difficult* to deal with, the consultee may find the results frustrating, feel like a failure, and drop out of the program.

The consultant should be a reinforcing person who gives the consultee frequent verbal rewards for his/her efforts in starting the program and for various steps in implementing it.

7. *Consider the different levels of expertise of consultees.* One of the biggest difficulties with group training is the wide variation in the level of expertise of members. One way to combat this problem is through individualizing instruction as discussed earlier. A pretest to determine which skill areas the consultee needs help with and a plan for him/her to attend only the sessions relevant to his/her needs will help gear the training to individuals. Also, choices of ways to become familiar with information may be made available. While one consultee may enjoy reading and find this is the best way to learn, another may prefer a lecture or a film or a tape. While it would be difficult and almost impossible to gear each training program to the specific needs of consultees, there could be some flexibility in methods used.

In addition to the above training tips, other concerns which need to be addressed in order to run an effective in-service training program include the following (Houmes, 1974):

1. Necessary information to be covered and the way of delivering this information;

2. The best time for training, group size, and facilities;

3. Participants interests, expectations, involvement and inter-
    action, and

4. Follow-up.

To help the consultant check himself or herself on these various
considerations, the Planning Checklist developed by Houmes may be
helpful.

Table 10: **Inservice Training for Change: Planning Checklist***

1. Have the goals and purposes been clearly stated?
2. Have outcomes been specified in performance terms?
3. Has preliminary information been made available to participants?
4. Has there been a structured opportunity to enable participants to review preliminary information?
5. Is the cognitive burden of the participants light?
6. Is the time appropriate (time of day, year)?
7. Is the time appropriate in regard to stimuli within the school, the district or the community which could work against a change orientation?
8. Has the optimum size of the in-service group(s) been determined?
9. Are the physical facilities conducive to training?
10. Does the program format make the participant performance expectations clear?
11. Will the training format enable participants to become actively involved?
12. If a consultant is to be used, is there a program provision for participants to interact individually with the consultant?
13. Are the training activities consistent with the established purpose, and are those activities aware of the participant interests?
14. Has responsibility been clearly assigned for leading the in-service program?
15. Has provision been made for post-training follow up, feedback and for planning the next steps?

Deal With Specific Problems of Implementation

There are four basic skills which can prove very valuable in
helping a consultee implement a program. First, the consultee needs
instructions or general information on what to do. Secondly, s/he

---

*Reprinted by permission from G. Houmes. "Revitalizing inservice training for change."
Educational Technology, 1974, XIX, 33-39.

needs a model to go by so that the desirable behavior to be emulated is seen by the consultee. If the behavior cannot be reproduced by the consultee, then shaping should be used. That is, the consultant sets several short-range sequenced goals which will lead to the desired behavior, and then rewards the consultee for achieving each of these step-wise goals. And, finally, the consultant can use prompts or cues to get the consultee to exhibit behaviors necessary for successful implementation of the program.

Instructions

Training may sometimes need to go back to the first step of an intervention, i.e., naming the specific problem. If the problem cannot be stated specifically, more observation may be warranted. If, on the other hand, it can be identified specifically, the consultant may then help the consultee identify which behaviors need to be increased and which decreased. Then s/he can give the consultee general ideas about how to increase or decrease behavior. For example:

Consultant: Exactly what is Jill doing that bothers you?

Consultee: She walks around the room a lot, stopping to talk with various kids. She'll tap them on the head with her pencil or poke them in the arms and they seem annoyed by her behavior. She seems to want to make friends but doesn't know how. On the playground before school, she chases the boys and hits them with her lunch box. She thinks they like it but they complain to me about it.

Consultant: OK, so you would like her to stay in her seat more, stop hitting kids with her pencil or lunch box and maybe learn ways of getting along with others.

Consultee: Right! Those are the things I'm concerned about.

Consultant: Actually, three techniques may be involved here. The in-seat behavior should be increased, the hitting behavior should be decreased, and in the case of Jill's social skills, these may need to be taught. It sounds like she just doesn't have the necessary skills.

Consultee: I don't think she does. I never would have thought about increasing or decreasing behavior. What difference does it make?

Consultant: There are some techniques which are very effective for decreasing behavior but which wouldn't be effective for increasing behavior. People usually do things more often if they receive a payoff for them. For instance, if your principal comes by and tells you how happy she is with your learning centers, you're likely to use them more often, aren't you?

Consultee: Sure. I'd probably even make some others.

Consultant: Okay, so the payoff makes the behavior increase. You would make sure, then, that you give a child some payoff when s/he behaves the way you want him/her to, in this case when Jill stays in her seat. You could not use this, however, for the poking and hitting behavior because you want to decrease it. In this case, you could either give a payoff for incompatible behavior, e.g., cooperating with peers, or give some adverse stimulus for the behavior, you don't like. For instance, when she hits others, she may lose a privilege she enjoys.

Consultee: Maybe recess.

Consultant: Yes, that would be a possibility if you know she enjoys recess.

Consultee: She does but this goes back to what we talked about earlier. She just doesn't know how to act with other kids.

Consultant: OK, there is still a third technique we'll have to try. In cases where the child doesn't know how to act, s/he has to be taught. You can't increase behaviors which aren't there to begin with.

The teacher may then be instructed to make a list of the specific behaviors s/he'd like the child to exhibit. If they are not operationalized, the consultant can teach him/her how to do so. Then specific instructions concerning the particular intervention method can be given. It is useful to recognize that in giving instructions, the consultant should use the vocabulary of the consultee and should state instructions in terms of suggestions rather than commands. Stating that "Praising the child for being in his/her seat is likely to make him/her want to stay in his/her seat more" is likely to be less objectionable to the teacher than, "You just be sure to praise him/her every time s/he is in his/her seat. Otherwise, you cannot expect any changes."

Modeling

In some cases, providing instructions to the consultee is not enough. In these cases the consultee must be shown how to use the skills with the client. This means that the consultant may have to show the consultee how to implement the skill.

Before the consultant models the skill, (s)he should go over the instructions with the consultee and make the consultee aware of what to look for. In some cases, the consultee can make the model's behavior more salient by signaling with his/her hand or raising his/her voice to let the consultee know what is coming. A sample typescript of a model demonstration of positive parental behavior is given below. The mother in this case watched the counselor reinforce cooperative behavior. Cooperative behavior was defined as taking one's turn in a game and sharing any materials necessary for the game to continue. Hands up signaled praise and hands down signaled ignoring or corrective feedback.

Consultant: Okay. It's your turn.

Child: Do I draw a card?

Consultant: (Signals with hand to mother) Yes, I like the way you ask questions. You are going to do well in this game.

Child: Oh, darn, it's your turn. I bet you're going to win. (Throws the dice down on the board).

Consultant: (Hand signal down, picks the dice up, rolls dice and moves marker four spaces) Now, it's your turn.

Child: (Rolls dice) I'll draw a card. I must give you ten points. (Hands a card to the consultant).

Consultant: (Hand signal up) Good! Now you are getting the hang of it.

When this short demonstration ended, the consultant asked the mother if she had any questions. Since she didn't the consultant summarized the modeled skills.

Consultant: Notice how I praised him when he asked questions about how to play and when he followed directions and gave me the card. I attempted to ignore him when he threw the dice.

The consultant can discuss alternative responses the parent might make in a similar situation and then provide the opportunity to practice the skills with the child.

Shaping

In some cases, the consultee may not be able to imitate what is modeled. Consequently, the consultant would need to break down the skills into simpler units and then reinforce successive approxima tions to the desired behavior. For example, a mother may be able to reinforce her child when s/he passes her a card but be unable to reward him/her when s/he takes his/her proper turn or asks relevant questions. In this case, the consultant should reinforce initial efforts (e.g., praise for the child when s/he gave him/her the card). Once the consultee is able consistently to praise the child's sharing, s/he can begin to reward taking turns and asking relevant questions. By establishing specific criterion levels for consultee performance, the consultee is able to remember the precise nature of the reinforce- ment response at each stage in the program and consequently can be reinforced consistently.

Prompting

Even though teachers may possess the necessary information to implement programs, they may not follow through as well as might be desired. Practice is often needed to actually put techniques into common use, and it would be very difficult for a teacher to suddenly change approaches without falling back into old patterns. This is where prompts can be useful in training.

Prompts can be either physical or verbal and essentially become discriminative stimuli or reminders of desirable behaviors the teacher should be exhibiting. For instance, if the teacher's task is to respond immediately to positive or pro-social behaviors in a child, the con- sultant can help make this happen by giving prompts. Of course, prompts are not to be used if not needed. They are beneficial when the consultee is having difficulty in consistently carrying out an intervention. The prompts can serve as signals to emit the desired behavior and at the same time help teach the consultee *when* to emit the behavior. An example of the use of prompts was given in the script on modeling where the consultant used hand signals to identify when the child should or should not be reinforced.

Fading out Models, Prompts, and Reinforcers

While models and prompts are often necessary in teaching new behaviors, the ultimate goal is for the desirable behavior to be emitted spontaneously. Consequently, while the goal behavior may be consistently reinforced, the discriminative stimuli which cue this behavior need to be gradually decreased. In the example where the consultant gives hand signals, the consultant initially models positive parental behavior. Following this, if the consultee is unable to emit the desirable behavior, the consultant provides prompts. These prompts should be lessened across parent/child interactions, however, until they can be eliminated entirely, with the consultee still emitting the desirable behavior. A good tip to follow is to give prompts just often enough to bring about the desired response and then to decrease them gradually. The decrease is important to keep the consultee from becoming dependent on models and prompts.

It is also important for the consultant to gradually thin out reinforcers. The consultant may initially wish to reinforce *all* desirable behavior. As this behavior becomes better established, however, it is more likely to be maintained if it is intermittently reinforced. Again, this decrease in reinforcers should be gradual. For example, in the training phase, the consultant may reinforce the consultee for every desirable response. As the consultee becomes more proficient, every single response is not likely to be praised. Rather, reinforcement would be contingent upon a series of good responses.

Evaluate Training

Evaluation has been considered throughout this chapter and in fact is a crucial part of an effective in-service training program. Emphasis has consistently been placed on pre-post data to determine participants' understanding or comprehension of information presented. Even more focus has been given to practice of skills presented and follow-up contacts to determine whether or not the skills are being implemented. Consequently, by following the suggested procedures, evaluative data would be available to answer the following questions:

1. Do the participants understand the information presented?

2. Can they perform the skills in a simulated setting? and finally,

3. Can they implement the skills in a real setting?

The first question can be answered with an evaluation instrument to determine whether or not participants learned the information presented. This, then, is a test of cognitive understanding. Information should also be obtained to measure the extent to which the methods and procedures used were effective in meeting program objectives. Attention should be given to assessing the following factors which are likely to affect program success:

1.   Environmental conditions (seating arrangements, lighting, room temperature).

2.   Amount of discussion time.

3.   Program presentation.

4.   Available resources.

5.   Supplies and equipment.

6.   Structure (small group, large group, individual work).

Sample questions for evaluating the program appear below:

1.   The program leader(s) presented the material clearly.

          yes   no

2.   There was adequate time for questions.

          yes   no

In addition to questions such as these, each participant could be asked what s/he would be doing differently as a result of this program.   Then these responses could be used to modify future programs and to evaluate changes that were brought about by the program.

It is important to get participant feedback on how they liked the workshop and it is also important to determine whether they can demonstrate the modeled skills in a simulated setting. However, the crucial evaluation is whether the skills can and will be implemented in a real setting, and only when this question can be answered affirmatively can the leader feel confident that a training program has been successful.

CONSULTING SKILLS INVENTORY

Directions: After each item, check (✓) "yes" or "no" to indicate whether the skill has been demonstrated.

Training The Consultee	*Yes*	*No*
1. Determine whether the consultee has training needs	____	____
(a) Deficiency in skills?	____	____
(b) Deficiency in motivation?	____	____
2. Determine training needs	____	____
3. Provide training	____	____
4. Attend to training tips	____	____
5. Deal with specific problems of implementation	____	____
6. Evaluate training	____	____

Criterion Test

Directions:

Given the following training program, specify objectives for each session and outline the activities for meeting those objectives.

Four teachers approached the counselor-consultant and asked for some help with children who were rejected. These children appeared to have no social skills and would not get involved in classroom activities. The teachers indicated that they would be interested in a social skills program for these students.

Possible Answer:

Session One: **Operationalizing Behavior**

Objective:

Each teacher will be able to write an operational description of "social rejection."

Activities:

Each teacher will be given a set of exercises to help him/her differentiate between labels and behaviors which refer to those labels. Once each teacher is able to write behavioral descriptions for each label, s/he will be asked to write down two or more behaviors for "social rejection."

The following behaviors are possibilities:

1. Standing by one's self while others are playing.
2. Failure to initiate conversations.
3. Entering an ongoing game without asking.
4. Starting to talk before others are finished.

Session Two: **Observing and Recording Behavior**

Objectives:

1. Given a video tape of child interaction, participants will be able to record the frequency of pre-specified behaviors with eighty percent reliability.
2. Given a recording sheet and graph paper, participants will be able to graph the frequency of pre-specified behaviors with ninety percent reliability.

Activities:

This session will begin with a review of the previous session. The participants will be given the rationale for observing and recording behavior. Each participant will be given recording paper and asked to record each instance of "positive interaction statements." They will then be taught to graph the data. Following this, each participant will specify the two target behaviors they listed the previous week and discuss how they would observe and record these behaviors.

Sessions Three and Four: Becoming familiar with Materials Designed to Teach and Provide Practice in Social Skills.

Objective:

Participants will be able to answer a ten question test concerning materials for teaching social skills to children with at least ninety percent accuracy.

Activities:

A package of materials about teaching skills to children will be demonstrated. The four steps of the teaching process will be introduced and participants will read the instructions for each skill, see the model tape, practice the skill themselves, and give each other feedback.

Session Five: Practice in Using the Packaged Materials

Objective:

Given four students, each participant will be able to implement the use of the social skills materials with a rating of "satisfactory" or better. The rating will be given by the workshop leader.

Activities:

Four students (or perhaps participants who are role-playing students) will be assigned to each participant. The participant will act as leader for the social skills training and implement this training in a manner similar to the one in which s/he participated in the two prior sessions.

9

MOTIVATING THE CONSULTANT AND CONSULTEE

It is quite encouraging when a consultant and consultee plan an effective behavior change program and even more encouraging when they begin implementing the program. Yet, these steps alone are not enough. Beyond these, it is crucial that reinforcers be available to *maintain* the initial consultee and consultant behavior and that these behaviors continue until the client's desirable behavior has become stable. In the end, many consultation programs fail because adequate reinforcers are unavailable to the consultee and the consultant. That is, the consultee's and/or consultant's behavior is often controlled by the same source of social reinforcement as that of the client; and unless the client, consultant, and consultee receive reciprocal payoff for their behavior, the positive effects of the program will be unlikely to maintain. Thus, in planning the program, the consultant and consultee should attempt to identify reinforcers for both consultee and consultant which will likely maintain throughout the program.

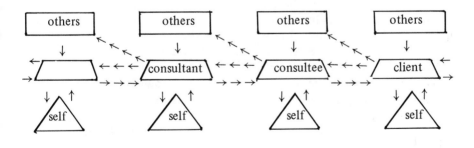

Figure 22: **Sources of Reinforcement for the Consultant and Consultee**

Sources of reinforcement for the consultee are: (1) the reinforcement which is under the control of the consultant; (2) the reinforcement from others surrounding the consultee (husband, teacher, employer, peer, etc.) (Tharp and Wetzel, 1969). These sources are shown graphically in Figure 22.

However, when the consultee is the focus, there is a third source of reinforcement to the consultee and that comes from the client (child). The modification of the client's behavior is a reinforcing event for the consultee.

Since reinforcers for changing the behavior of the client have been adequately discussed this will not be addressed here. Instead, this chapter will deal with reinforcers to maintain the positive behavior of the consultee and the consultant.

Identify sources of Reinforcement for Consultee

In attempting to identify sources of reinforcement for the consultee, the consultant and consultee should first look for rewards and incentives which currently exist in the environment. One investigation (Kimball, 1974) of schools showed that teachers in schools with high student achievement reported intrinsic rewards for their work more frequently than would be expected. These self-assigned rewards included a sense of personal achievement, increased self-confidence, and satisfaction in a job well done. On the other hand, teachers in schools where student achievement was low reported formal, extrinsic rewards (job security, salary increases, encouragement, etc.) as incentives more frequently than would be expected.

Since the intrinsic reinforcers naturally occur in the school environment, how does the consultant identify them? For example, if the consultee is trying to change client attendance or achievement, how does the consultant know whether these events are reinforcing to the consultee? One way to find out is through the consultee's behavior. If the consultee fails to implement the program properly or complains about the amount of time the program is taking, then behavior change in itself is not reinforcing. In this case, the amount of time the consultant is spending on implementing the program is of more interest to the consultee than the positive changes in the client's behavior.

Another approach which can help identify whether behavior change is intrinsically reinforcing is for the consultant to illustrate graphically the positive changes in the client's behavior (improved achievement, attendance, etc.) and the decreasing amount of time the consultee is attending to the client's inappropriate behavior.

Often the consultant can detect a smile or enthusiasm in how the consultee responds to the illustrated changes. Or, often the consultant can detect the consultee's dissatisfaction.

Consultant: I have graphed Edna's scores for the last week. Does it seem we have reached our objective?

Teacher: Yes, but it seems like she is still not working up to her ability.

In this case, the consultee does not appear satisfied or reinforced by the successful completion of the objective. Perhaps a new objective should be established as well as identifying any conditions which may impede proper implementation of the program.

Consultant: So even though we reached our objective, you feel she could do more.

Teacher: Yes, she has a lot of spare time and spends a lot of it talking with others.

Consultant: What if we set another objective and ask her to do more work?

Teacher: Well. OK.

Consultant: Are you wondering whether it is worth it?

The teacher in this instance may not be adequately reinforced by the client's improved performance. Here the consultant might consider other sources of reinforcement.

Teacher: Yes, I don't know whether she can ever stop her talking long enough to work up to her capacity.

Consultant: These changes will take time. She seems to complete more assignments when you give her positive comments. I've noticed that you've worked hard recently to give her positive comments for desirable behavior.

Here the consultant is reinforcing the consultee. The consultant might also encourage the consultee by telling him/her how the program might be carried out. Likewise, the consultant might visit the classroom in the early stages and give positive comments to the consultee for following through on these plans.

In other cases, the consultant may have to rely on others to provide reinforcement to the consultee. Some behaviors, such as self-help skills in severely and profoundly retarded children, are acquired very gradually (Panyon, Boozer, & Morris, 1970). In these cases, reinforcement for the consultee's behavior in terms of the client's progress is often delayed. Therefore, the performance of consultees who work with retarded or emotionally disturbed children might require special reinforcers (e.g., comments about good training behaviors). Contingent application of a combination of these reinforcers can increase the amount of interaction between consultee and client. In providing potent reinforcers, however, the consultant must know who is reinforcing or important to the consultee. For example, in some cases, the principal may be the most reinforcing individual to the consultee (teacher), so the consultant could show the principal a report or graph of the client's improved behavior and ask him/her to make some positive comments to the teacher. Likewise, the principal could be asked to drop by each day to observe the program being implemented. Positive comments such as, "This really looks like it's working" or questions such as "How much work has s/he completed today?" may prove to be effective reinforcers in the teacher's implementation of the program.

The consultant might also work with the principal in developing a newsletter which would give recognition to those teachers who are working on special projects. Teachers who are working with special problems or are trying new procedures could be featured. These articles could also be sent to the local newspaper. The newsletter would provide added opportunities for school personnel and the community to reward the teacher's accomplishments.

In addition to newsletters, visitation programs could be established within and between buildings. Consultants could provide relief for teachers who wish to demonstrate a new procedure with other interested teachers. This not only frees up the teacher for outside activities but places him/her in a new role as a peer supervisor.

If the principal is unpopular with the teacher, s/he would be an inappropriate source of reinforcement to the consultee. In this instance, the consultant should attempt to identify other reinforcing individuals in the consultee's environment, e.g., other teachers whose opinions or relationship the teacher values. Often the consultant can determine these relationships through close observation. For instance, with whom does the teacher talk in the hallways, playground, lounge, etc.? With whom does the teacher share materials or instruction?

The above procedures are most useful when the consultant works within the institution. For consultants who work in agencies and mental health centers outside the consultee institution, other procedures such as questionnaires can be identified. Questionnaires should identify people and activities which are reinforcing to the consultee.

Sample Questionnaire

1. I feel good about myself when my child (student) is _____
    _____

2. When I have problems with my child (student), I generally talk with
    _____

3. Whom do you feel works most positively with your child (student)?
    _____

4. What activities do you enjoy the most?_____
    _____

5. Whom do you enjoy doing these activities with?_____
    _____

6. The teacher (parent) I wish I were more like is _____
    _____

7. I usually attend parent (teacher) conferences with _____
    _____

8. The best teacher (parent) I know is _____
    _____

9. Children are a source of inspiration to me when _____
    _____

10. When I am with my children (students), I like to_____
    _____

Once the consultant identifies reinforcing activities and people for the consultee, s/he should attempt to incorporate these into the program/contract (Tharp, 1975).

In addition to selecting reinforcing persons, another task of the consultant is to determine reinforcing events for the consultee. One strategy which has been successful in this area is a values auction. Essentially, the person or persons involved in the exercise choose from a list of possible events the ones of greatest value to them and then bid accordingly. Table 11 is a list of values or events which could be included in the auction.

Table 11: **Teacher Values**

Items To Be Auctioned	Amount Budgeted	Highest Amount Bid	Won
1. Recognition at faculty meetings for good teaching			
2. $15 worth of classroom resource materials			
3. A day off from regular lunchroom duty			
4. Pat on the back and compliment from the principal			
5. A day off from hall duty			
6. A teacher aide for two hours per week			
7. Recognition of good teaching at a PTA meeting			
8. A day off from bus duty			
9. Compliments from two students about your teaching			
10. Getting to go home immediately after school for one week			
11. Having a free (planning) period each day for one week			
12. A day off from recess duty			
13. A chance to attend a two day workshop on teaching methods			
14. Permission to get classroom materials from the public library (on school time)			
15. A chance to organize a faculty party			
16. A chance to transfer one pupil from your room			

By identifying the things the consultee bids on, the consultant can readily determine some possible reinforcers for him/her.

Checklists similar to that of the values auction can be used in other ways also. For example, the consultee may rank order the events in terms of their interest and value or may simply write fifteen or twenty things which s/he would like to see happen at school, home, within the institution, etc.

Tharp & Wetzel (1969) suggest that the same analyses which were performed on the client may be used to assess sources of reinforcement controlling the consultee's behavior. For example, a teacher may individualize instruction and thus improve the client's behavior (+) but increase the noise level because of students moving to and from learning situations (−). This noise may be disapproved of by the principal. It is possible, then, that the consultee's behavior is more influenced by the principal's disapproval than the client's improved academic behavior, thereby reducing the probability of continuing the program. On the other hand, if the teacher were more influenced by the client's improved grades than the principal's disapproval, s/he would likely continue implementing the program. Its continuation would be even more insured, however, if the teacher across the hall were excited about the program and wanted the consultee to help organize learning centers (+).

If the consultant and consultee select target behaviors which will have potential benefit to more individuals (principal, teacher, social worker, etc.) than the people immediately involved, the consultee can maximize the positive feedback s/he will likely receive from others.

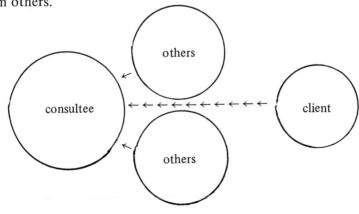

Figure 23: **Diagram of Positive Feedback to Consultee**

Exercise: **Reinforcement for Consultee**

Directions: List two other possible sources of reinforcement that could maintain a mother's behavior in the following situations.

A mother may spend time with her son while he is playing quietly and this "makes her feel good" (+) but her husband is annoyed because she sometimes doesn't talk with him (−).

1. _____

2. _____

Suggested Answers:

1. Consultant's positive comments for successful implementation.

2. Drinking a cup of coffee, listening to a record for each fifteen minutes her sons play quietly.

Identify Sources of Reinforcement for the Consultant

The same principles of reinforcement that work for the consultee and client also apply to the consultant. The sources of positive consultant behavior are: (1) improved consultee performance or adequate implementation of the program, and (2) positive comments by peers and colleagues.

In order to be positively reinforced by the consultee, the consultant must be a source of influence for the consultee. This may sometimes be difficult because the consultant sometimes does not have the needed creditability, i.e., the consultee may think s/he will get little help from the consultant. In other cases, where the consultant may have worked in the school or agency for a long period of time, a close personal relationship may prevent the consultant from performing at his/her best. A sample of effective consulting behavior follows:

Consultant: Let's look at the graph and see if we reached our objective.

Teacher: Well, I guess not. He didn't do any of his work on Thursday or Friday. Maybe I should have given him more attention the other days. I see I missed several opportunities but you can't imagine what it's like in here. I have no time. You know how it is. You taught here last year.

Consultant: I know Bill. Why don't you do what you can?

Here, it may help for a different consultant to take over the case. If the consultants work out of a mental health center or agency, they can be rotated. In this way, the consultant can be less susceptible to consultee excuses and can set up conditions so the consultee is more likely to respond and be successful in changing client behavior. This client behavior change then will result both in reinforcement for the consultee and the consultant.

Another source of reinforcement for the consultant is his/her supervisor. In agencies, the consultant can increase the likelihood of receiving approval from the supervisor by asking advice on specific cases, present written case reports, or setting up case conferences where supervisors have an opportunity to comment on the consultant's behavior.

The sources of reinforcement are somewhat different in a school system. Supervisors are often not located in the school. Instead, the consultant often reports to a principal who wants results but does not have training in consulting. Here the consultant can set up a meeting with the supervisor (e.g., pupil personnel director) and building principal. Role relationships can be established, and a mechanism (case conferences, reports, etc.) for disseminating information can be discussed.

Another major source of reinforcement is one's peers or colleagues. Professionals find the need to discuss problems with colleages to whom they can present their cases and receive constructive feedback. Since a school often may employ only one counselor/consultant, a network of communication to discuss cases must be established. Professional meetings and small group meetings of counselor/consultants at adjoining schools can be used to discuss special problems which relate to the consultant's role.

Exercise: **Reinforcement for Consultant**

Directions: List two sources of reinforcement that will likely maintain the consultant's desire to work with the parent in the following situation.

A consultant has worked for three weeks with a parent on effective parenting techniques. S/he is now observing this parent interact with his/her child at home.

1. _____

2. _____

Suggested Answers:

1. Positive comments from the parent suggesting that the program is helpful.

2. Positive comments from other colleagues.

Identify Sources of Reinforcement for Self

It is possible to enhance the effectiveness and maintenance of a treatment program by teaching the child, consultee, and consultant to identify sources of influence for themselves.   Tharp (1975) suggests that self-congratulations and comparison of achievements with past performance can serve as a source of reinforcement to the self.   One way to accomplish this is for each party to record his/her own performance (number of contacts, amount of time, etc.).   Then, the consultant, consultee, and client can compare their performances with an objective or self-held standard.   If the objective is reached or exceeded, the individual will likely feel good about it and continue to maintain his/her standard of performance.   For example, if a mother is able to encourage her child to interact positively with others, she may "feel good" about her behavior and tell herself she is being a good mother.

Exercise: Self-reinforcement

Directions: Identify two sources of self-reinforcement for a parent in a consultation program.

1. _____
2. _____

Suggested Answers:

1. Comparing his/her behavior with a pre-specified objective.

2. Saying, "I'm a good mother/father."

In the final analysis, it is the success or failure of the consultant to involve consultees in effective behavior change programs which determines whether or not his/her consulting experiences are continued or dropped. If s/he is usually successful in getting the consultee involved in planning and implementing programs, there is payoff for him/her. If the consultee does not follow through or seems disinterested in consulting services, consulting attempts are likely to be extinguished. If time constraints require the consultant to set priorities on cases, then, the consultant should first select consultees and behaviors which have the best potential for positive consequences. The result then will be more positive feelings toward the consulting role and greater maintenance of desirable consultee, consultant, and client behaviors.

Criterion Test

1. In the following diagram, draw the appropriate arrows, indicating sources of influence among consultant, consultee, client, and others.

2. A teacher is implementing some group activities which will increase interaction with a group of social isolates. List two sources of reinforcement that would likely maintain his/her level of desirable behavior.

    (a)————————————————————————————————

    (b)————————————————————————————————

3. A consultant is spending time observing teacher-pupil interaction in the classroom. List two sources of reinforcement that will likely maintain his/her level of desirable behavior.

    (a)————————————————————————————————

    (b)————————————————————————————————

4. Identify two sources of self-reinforcement for a teacher in a consultation program.

    (a)————————————————————————————————

    (b)————————————————————————————————

Criterion Test Answers

1.

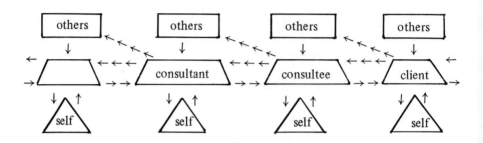

2.   (a)   positive comments from the consultant or others

(b)   student's increased social participation

3.   (a)   improved teacher performance

(b)   positive comments by teacher

4.   (a)   principal

(b)   consultant

CONSULTING SKILLS INVENTORY

Directions: After each item, check [√] "yes" or "no" to indicate whether the skill has been demonstrated.

MOTIVATING CONSULTANT and CONSULTEE	YES	NO
1. Identify sources of reinforcement for the consultee.	[ ]	[ ]
2. Identify sources of reinforcement for the consultant.	[ ]	[ ]
3. Identify sources of reinforcement for self.	[ ]	[ ]

10

EVALUATING CONSULTATION

Evaluation of the consultation process is based on the successful completion of objectives which have been stated in measurable terms. Data (observations, test scores, etc.) about the client collected during consultation provide the consultant and consultee with the necessary information to determine whether the objectives have been met.

Determine If Outcome Objectives Have Been Met

Evaluating Objectives for Consultation

In the goal setting phase, the consultant often sets general, subordinate, and performance objectives. In the evaluation phase, then, each of these goals is measured for level of attainment. That is, the consultant and consultee may have specified a hierarchy of objectives and several subordinate goals will have to be completed before the ultimate goal can be achieved. For example, the client will likely not be able to give information about himself/herself or get information from others unless s/he can initiate a conversation. It makes sense, then, that subordinate goal attainment will be monitored and the evaluation becomes an ongoing process rather than just a post-treatment measure.

In discussing objectives, the consultant and consultee should consider each one separately (Bergan, 1977). The interview may begin with the consultant asking the consultee to examine the data pertaining to the first objective.

Consultant: Lets look at the observation sheet for Jack.

Teacher: Okay. I have it right here.

Consultant: You said you would check each time Jack initiated a positive interaction with someone and write down the time and the person he contacted.

Teacher: Yes. I have it right here.

Next, the consultant should state the objective as it was written in the program script.

> Consultant: OK. We said that Jack should initiate three conversions each day for one week.
>
> Teacher: Right.

Once the data is collected, the consultant should ask the consultee whether the objective has been met.

> Consultant: Allright, judging from your observation sheet, do you think Jack has met the objective.
>
> Teacher: Let's see . . . it looks like he has . . . he has at least three initiated contacts.

If the objective has been met the consultant and consultee can go on to the next objective. Otherwise discussion must focus on why the objective has not been met. It is critical not to switch discussion from one objective to the next since this often creates confusion.

If the initial objective (e.g., initiating positive interactions) has been met, the consultant might ask the consultee if s/he wishes to write a new performance objective (e.g., initiate one conversation with a stranger each day for one week) for the first subordinate objective (e.g., initiating a conversation). If not, the consultant and consultee should consider the next subordinate objective and see if any adjustments need to be made in the objective (e.g., changing the criterion level or conditions) or the program (e.g., changing the procedures to reach the objective). In addition, the consultant and consultee may want to add subordinate objectives (e.g., improve problem solving abilities) to increase the chances that the general outcome goal will be reached (e.g., develop social interaction skills).

If the goal attainment scaling process has been used, the consultant and consultee can rate the client's behavior at the end of the specified time period and determine the level of goal attainment, e.g., expected level, less than expected, or more than expected.

Criterion Levels Met?

Successful completion of objectives is often predicated on the client reaching the desired level of performance. In order to determine whether the client has reached the desired level of performance, the consultant must develop an appropriate evaluation design. An evaluation design specifies *when* and *what* data will be collected.

Evaluating Behavioral Changes

There are a variety of evaluation designs the consultant may utilize. The most useful for evaluating specific behavioral changes are time series designs where data are collected over different points in time. Some of these designs have been developed for experimental purposes and therefore may not be practical for the consultant and consultee who in many cases must change the client's behavior in the shortest period of time. Only those designs which are of practical use to the consultant will be discussed in this chapter. Readers who are interested in a more detailed analysis of time series designs should consult Schmidt (1974).

AB Design

The simplest of the time series designs is the AB Designs. Here the consultant and consultee first record baseline rates of target behaviors (positive social interactions, test scores, etc.). Based upon the baseline level of behavior, the consultant and consultee and possibly the client set an objective. It is helpful to specify the number of consecutive days the criterion must be achieved to provide an objective determination of when the criterion has been met. The consultant gathers a second set of data during the implementation phase of the program. Data may be collected continuously throughout the program or collected at specific times throughout the following implementation of the program. For example, during baseline Jim was only completing sixty percent of his assignments. Based on this assessment the consultant and teacher initially set a goal that Jim would complete eighty percent of his assignments after one week. During the second week Jim could be a line leader for each day he completed eighty percent of his assignments. Figure 24 shows that Jim completed ninety percent of his assignments after the second week. The consultant and teacher agreed that the objective was met.

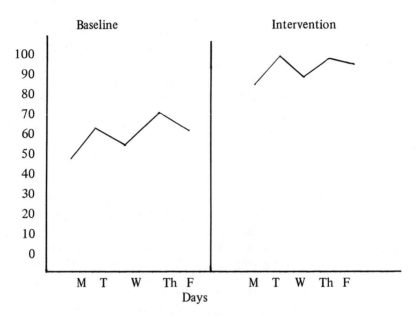

Percentage Assignments Completed

Figure 24: **AB Design (One Intervention)**

By graphing the data the consultant and teacher can set realistic objectives and monitor objectives on a daily basis.

The AB Design in the instance provides the consultant and consultee an easy means of evaluating one behavior of one client in one setting. The consultant may only need to collect baseline data for several days (until there is some consistency in the rate) then set a reasonable objective and continue collecting data to measure changes.

The consultant should be mindful that other events might also be influencing behavior of the client. For example, while the teacher allowed Jim to be a line leader each day, Jim may have been getting better grades or encouragement from his parents or other children. However, despite the fact that this design does not control for error resulting from competing events, it is an acceptable means for determining whether an objective has been met.

In some instances the consultant and consultee may wish to evaluate the effects of more than one intervention on client behavior. Once Jim had completed ninety percent of his assignments the consultant and teacher wanted to set a new objective whereby Jim would complete one hundred percent of his assignments four out of five days for the following week. This would involve adding a second intervention, then. In this case the teacher sent a note home with Jim each day he completed one hundred percent of his assignments. The note instructed the parents to compliment Jim on completing his work.

In Figure 25 one can see that when the second intervention was introduced Jim completed one hundred percent of his assignments only two of the five days. At this point, the teacher asked the parents to let Jim stay up one half hour later each night to watch TV for each note he brought home.

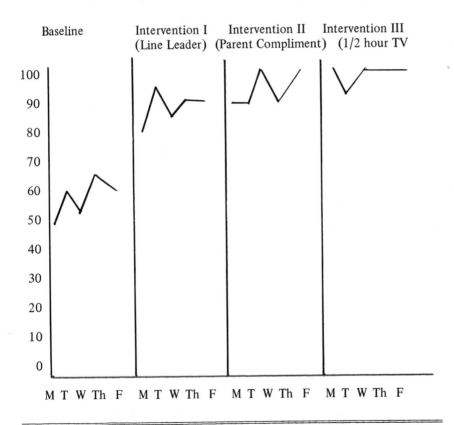

Figure 25: **AB Design (Three Interventions)**

When the third intervention was implemented Jim completed one hundred percent of his assignments four out of five days, thus meeting his objective.

Single Group Multiple Intervention Design

In the single group multiple intervention design, the consultant can easily evaluate the effects of more than one intervention. However, like the AB design, the single group multiple intervention design does not control for outside influences which also might have changed the client behavior. In addition, there may be cumulative effects of each intervention. That is, the effects of the first intervention may affect the second intervention and the third intervention (i.e. one half hour of television may have been enhanced by parent's compliments).

Exercise: Single Group Multiple Intervention Design

Directions: Given the objective and following the graph information in Figure 22, answer the questions following Figure 26.

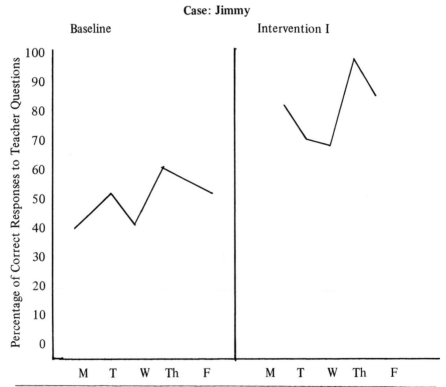

Figure 26: **Single Group Multiple Intervention Design**

Objective:

Jimmy will show a twenty percent average increase in correct responses to ten questions from baseline to the end of intervention I (end of second week).

1. What is being measured in Figure 26?

_____

2. a. What is the average percentage of correct responses during baseline?

_____

    b. During intervention?

_____

3. Did Jimmy meet his objective?

_____

Answers:

1. Percent of correct responses to teacher questions
2. (a) X = 48%
    (b) X = 78%
3. yes

Multiple Baseline

In some instances, the consultant and consultee may be interested in more than one target behavior for a particular client, or, s/he may want to measure changes on a specific problem for multiple clients or situations. This is referred to as the multiple baseline. For example, a second problem behavior for Jim in addition to not completing his assignments was his failure to eat breakfast or lunch.

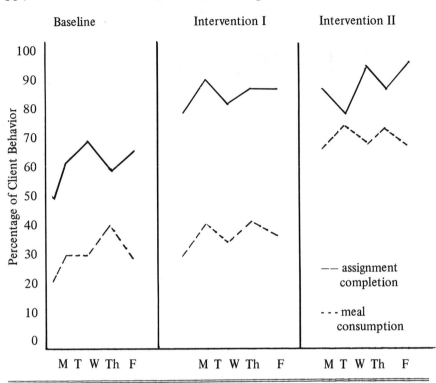

Figure 27: **Multiple Baseline Across Problems**

Figure 27 illustrates an increase in assignment completion when exposed to an intervention (i.e., line leader for each day eighty percent of assignments are completed) while meal consumption (which is not being treated) remains at its baseline level. When the first objective was met, the consultant and consultee set another objective to increase meal consumption by forty percent. In order to determine whether each meal was completed the teacher made a list of each food (milk, eggs, hamburger, etc.) and checked off when the meal was consumed. It also illustrates that meal consumption does not increase until the second intervention period when being a line leader is also made contingent on meal consumption. By exposing each target behavior (i.e., assignment completion and meal consumption) to the intervention, the consultant and consultee can determine if the intervention is actually responsible for meeting the objective. That is, each client behavior should change only as it is exposed to the intervention and not before. It should be noted that the multiple baseline across behaviors is inappropriate when target behaviors are related. For example, if talking out is related to turning around in seat, a decrease in one behavior would probably be associated with a decrease in the other.

In some cases, the consultant and consultee may be working with more than one client who has the same problem. For example, in addition to Jim, Eric may also be having problems with completing assignments. Figure 28 illustrates that during baseline, Jim's average level of assignment completion was sixty percent while Eric's average level of completion was fifty percent.

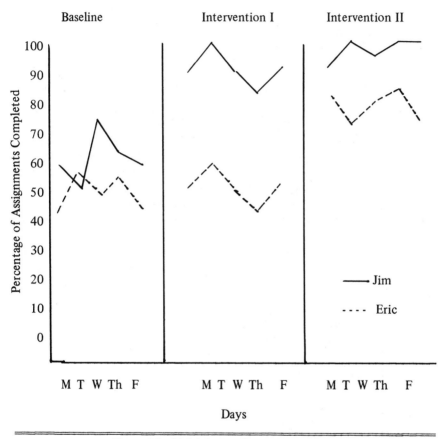

Figure 28: **Multiple Baseline Across Clients**

During the second week, Jim was exposed to an intervention and his assignment completion increased to ninety percent. At the same time, baseline conditions remained for Eric and his behavior showed little change ($\bar{x} = 55\%$). When Eric was exposed to the intervention, however, his assignment completion increased to an average level of seventy-five percent. This type of multiple baseline allows the consultant and consultee to determine the effectiveness of an intervent· ion in reaching their objective (e.g., completing assignments) for two clients.

While the purpose of the multiple baseline across clients is to determine whether client changes result from the intervention, there are sometimes competing forces which produce the change. For instance, if one student begins completing assignments, another student may simply imitate that behavior, irrespective of the intervention. Thus, where modeling is likely to occur, multiple baseline across clients designs are inappropriate.

There are many instances where the target behavior will occur in more than one situation (home, school, neighborhood, etc.). In this case, the consultant and consultee can use the multiple baseline to evaluate the target behaviors of a client concurrently in different situations. For example, while Jim may not be completing assignments at school, he also may not be completing assignments at home. Figure 29 shows that during the first week, Jim completed sixty percent ($\bar{x}$) of his assignments at school and forty percent ($\bar{x}$) at home. In the second week, an intervention was administered by the teacher at school and the average level of assignment completion increased to eighty percent while the average level of assignment completion at home increased slightly to fifty percent at baseline. There are times when multiple baseline across situations designs are inappropriate also. Some individual's behaviors are more likely to generalize from one setting to another.

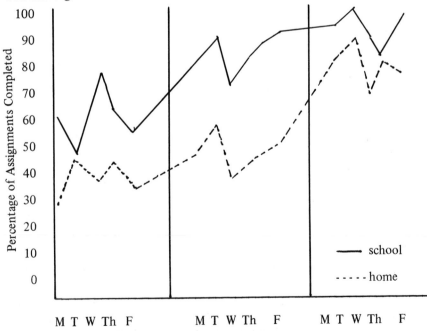

Figure 29: **Multiple Baseline Across Situations**

When an intervention was introduced by the parents at home during the third week, the average level of assignment completion increased to eighty percent. The multiple baseline here is useful in determining the success of an intervention when the problem occurs in more than one setting. In addition, by showing that the intervention affects more than one client, behavior, or setting at different points in time, it lends validity to the behavior change resulting from the intervention rather than other factors.

The major disadvantage with this design is that behavior change in one situation may be correlated with change in another situation. For example, increasing a client's social interaction in the classroom may also increase his/her social interaction on the playground in the absence of a specific intervention.

Exercise: **Multiple Baseline Across Situations**

Directions: Given the following graphic information, answer the questions following the graph.

Mary fails to comply with directions at home and school. The percentages of compliances are recorded below:

	Baseline	Intervention I	Intervention II
	M T W Th F	M T W Th F	M T W Th F
Home:	20 10 10 20 25	40 45 50 55 50	60 50 40 50 45
School:	15 20 30 20 25	15 20 25 20 30	40 50 55 60 50

Figure 30: **Graph To Be Completed**

1. Label and graph the data on the axes in Figure 30.

2. What is being measured in the preceding graph?

   _____ across_____

3. Where/for whom is the intervention being introduced in the first intervention period?

4. What target behavior is likely under the intervention in the second period?

5. Describe the change in percent of compliance from Baseline to Intervention II.

   Home _____

   School _____

6. In seventy-five words or less, describe the data presented in the graph.

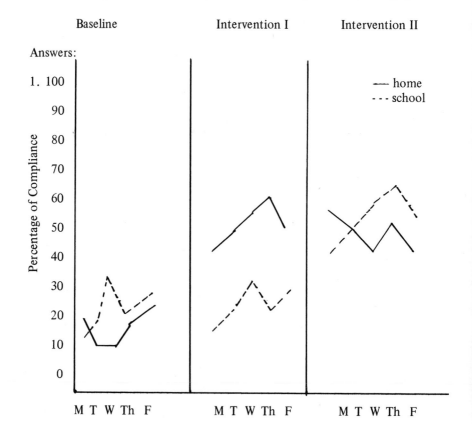

Answers:

1.

Figure 31: **Graph Completed**

* Figure 31 graph refers to Figure 30 graph.

2.   Compliance across situations.

3.   Home

4.   School

5.   School: More than doubled (a factor of 2.32)
      Home: More than tripled (a factor of 3.27)

6.   The percentage of compliance was measured for three weeks across home
      and school. At the start of the second week an intervention was introduced
      in the home and the percentage of compliance more than tripled (3.20)
      while little change occurred at school. During the third week, the per-
      centage of compliance at school more than doubled (2.32) the figure for
      baseline. In that third week, the percentage of compliance at home
      continued to increase.

Changing Criterion Design

The fourth and final time series design is the changing criterion design.
In this design a baseline is followed by implementation of the plan (i.e., intervention). The intervention is made contingent upon increasing levels of performance when behavior changes successfully at or close to the set criterion
levels, experimental control can be demonstrated (Sulzer-Azaroff and Mayer,
1977). For example, in Figure 32 the mother's praise is made contingent upon
the percentage of compliance behavior. Following baseline the consultant and
parent set an objective of at least sixty percent compliance each day for the
first week. When observational data indicates that the objective has been met,
the criterion for praise is changed to seventy percent per day for the third week.

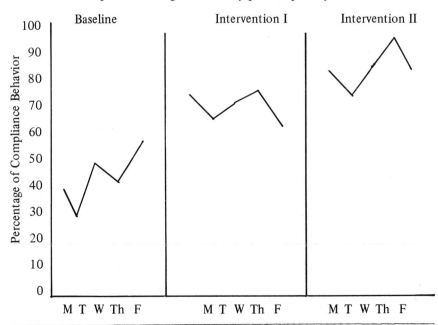

Figure 32: **Changing Criterion Design**

The changing criterion design is advantageous where the consultant and consultee do not expect marked changes in the client's behavior during the initial phase of the implementation plan (i.e., intervention). Such a design also prevents the consultant, teacher, or parent from setting unrealistic criterion levels of performance so that the client never receives the treatment (i.e. reinforcement). This design like the AB design fails to control for outside factors which also may be changing the client's behavior.

This design is most useful as a shaping procedure or way to reach approximations of the desired behavior. For example, a teacher may desire a child to complete seventy percent of his/her assignments one week, eighty percent the next week, ninety percent the next week, etc. Likewise, a parent may desire that a child comply with his/her demands eighty percent one week and ninety percent the next week.

Experimental control with this design may be lost if criterion levels are too close together or too far apart. For example, the criterion level may be too high for a social isolate who is able to initiate one conversation each day for one week but is unable to reach the criterion level of three conversations next week. Criterion levels should be set with care so that the client can reach his/her goal.

Evaluating Cognitive Changes

As indicated in Chapter Four, assessment of a child's academic abilities may be useful. Such assessment is typically made in order to determine the child's present skill level relative to others his/her age as well as in reference to a specified criterion. Once a child's skill level, learning style, etc. is determined, goals can be set accordingly. Again, these should be stated in measurable terms, e.g., following a unit of instruction (1) Billy will be able to say all the short and long vowel sounds with one hundred percent accuracy, (2) given a list of words, Billy will be able to identify all the initial and final consonant sounds. After Billy masters these skills, an additional subordinate objective will be established toward the ultimate goal of teaching him to read. Evaluation may be based on completion of objectives within the time frame specified in the objective.

Norm referenced measures can also be used as evaluative tools. Since many of these test scores (particularly achievement tests) are reported in grade equivalencies, one can assume that a child should progress one level during an academic year of instruction. Hence, if the goal is for the child to progress one level, or even to determine whether s/he has made greater improvement this year, his/her movement toward that objective can readily be measured with norm referenced tests.

Evaluating Affective Changes

Affective changes can be measured either by determining changes from baseline to end of treatment or by setting specific goals and measuring the level of attainment. For instance, Ms. Bell set a goal for a thirty-three percent increase in Carol's positive self-statements and a twenty percent decrease in her negative self-statements. Evaluation in this case involved both changes from baseline to post-treatment and specific goal attainment. Baseline data had to be determined in order to tell whether the behavior was increasing or decreasing, and the goal specified the expected degree of change. Affective changes in groups of students are often measured by pre-post change scores on attitude tests (e.g., attitude toward school), from self-esteem instruments (e.g., Piers-Harris or Coopersmith), etc. One difficulty with this approach, however, is the variety of intervening events which may account for the change. In addition, some of the changes may be due to maturity or developmental changes. Such threats to the validity of the data can be minimized by having a control group who receives no treatment. Then, if the gains for the experimental subjects are significantly greater than for the control subjects, one is safer in assuming that the intervention made the difference.

For measuring affective changes in an individual over time (baseline through interventions), the AB design discussed earlier can be used if the behavior is operationalized. For instance, if the behavior is operationalized as the number of positive interactions with peers, the child can be observed at a specified time each day and the behavior charted.

Maintaining The Program

When objectives have been met and no new objectives have been set the consultant, consultee and in some cases the client must determine how to maintain the desired changes in the client's behavior. This may be often necessary because old behaviors (fighting, name-calling, etc.) may reappear.

While it is important to prevent problem behaviors from re-appearing, it is also difficult for parents and teachers to maintain a program at its present level. Outside activities, fatigue and lack of support from the consultant often prevent parents and teachers from maintaining the initial program. Thus, it is often not practical for the consultant to ask the consultee to maintain the program without arranging for the program to be redesigned.

Intermittent Schedule of Reinforcement

There are two primary ways the consultant can help the consultee maintain the program without overburdening the consultee. First, the consultant could arrange for positive consequences (i.e. reinforcers) to be delivered to the child on an intermittent schedule of reinforcement. That is, rather than reinforce the teacher or parent on a fixed or daily schedule, the consultant would vary the reinforcement. For example, when the teacher or parent have been producing desired changes in the child over a two or three week period, the consultant might gradually begin to make fewer observations or schedule fewer meetings to discuss the child's progress. Likewise, meetings or observations could be scheduled on an intermittent or varied schedule to enhance the maintenance of the consultee's program. Here, the consultant could hold periodic group meetings with teachers and parents. Parents and teachers could be encouraged to reinforce each other for maintaining their programs.

These same procedures help to maintain desired levels of the client's behavior. For example, initially the teacher or parent might reinforce the child each time s/he behaves appropriately for 30 minutes. When the child's response pattern is stable, the parent or teacher can vary the amount of time they reinforce the child (every 15 minutes, then every 20 min., 30 min., etc.). In a sense, the teacher or parent is "surprising" the child with reinforcers rather than allowing the child to predict that s/he will always get a reinforcer after a specified number of appropriate responses (e.g., three, four, five) or for a specified amount of time (O'Leary & O'Leary, 1972). When the child is unable to predict when s/he will receive reinforcers, s/he will keep working longer to earn them.

Sulzer-Azaroff & Mayer (1977) recommend that the consultant reinforce the consultee enough to maintain the program. They suggest that if the consultant cannot contact the consultee at least once or twice a week during the implementation phase of the program, the program should not be started. If the consultant cannot meet directly with the consultee, then periodic phone calls or notes will likely maintain the program. These notes or calls often serve as reinforcers as well as prompts to keep the program going.

Reducing the Amount of Reinforcement

Consultant and client behavior can be maintained if the amount of reinforcement is gradually reduced. When a consultant tells a consultee s/he is happy with how s/he is maintaining the client's academic or social progress, s/he may smile or give him or her a pat on the back. When a teacher gives a child an "A" for a paper, s/he may smile at him/her. Once these nonverbal gestures have been paired with other reinforcers (positive comments, recognition, pay checks, etc.) to produce desired levels of consultee or client behavior, they alone can be used to maintain the program.

Another way to reduce the amount of reinforcement is to increase the frequency or amount of behavior for the same amount of reinforcement. For example, parents may deliver tokens for two, three, or four tasks completed. Ultimately, however, the child receives tokens only when all his/her tasks have been completed. Likewise, the cost for staying up late or going somewhere may increase.

Self Control

A second primary strategy for enhancing maintainance is to place the program under the control of the client. For example, Birkimer & Brown (1979) demonstrated that five children could be taught to maintain desirable levels of behavior after teacher reinforcement was withdrawn. The self-control program included five phases. The first phase consisted of a baseline to record the level of off-task behavior. Secondly, a set of rules was posted on the blackboard at the side of the room where each child could see them. In the third phase, the teacher administered a point system, giving each child a rating from zero (low) to ten (high) at the end of each session, depending upon the appropriateness of the child's behavior. Later in the day, children exchanged their points (rating) for any of the activity reinforcers they could afford. The fourth phase was the same as the third except that children rated their own behavior. At the end of the period each child told the teacher the rating s/he gave himself/herself and the teacher told the child the rating s/he had assigned. Children whose ratings were within plus or minus one point of the teacher's received two bonus points, while children who differed by more than one point lost two points. In the fifth and final phase, the teacher withdrew the reinforcement for the child's behavior. Even when teacher reinforcement was removed, the child's appropriate behavior maintained. This program likely leads the children to attend more closely to the adequacy of their behavior.

Likewise when a teacher or parent takes an active role in designing the intervention program, they are more likely to design a program which they will maintain. Parents and teachers can be taught to reward themselves for a job well done (Tharp & Wetzel, 1969). A cup of coffee, TV show or a break can be scheduled after the consultee has successfully implemented the program. Such reinforcers can be self-administered by the consultee to maintain the program.

Transfer of Learning

Another way to ensure maintenance is to implement the program in new settings. Unless an intervention plan is designed to insure generalization to new settings, generalization will likely not occur (Wahler, 1969). For example, a client may be taught how to interact positively with one individual but s/he may be unable to interact with others in a group. Likewise, a child may be able to follow directions at home but may not be able to follow directions at school. Thus, the consultant and consultee should discuss specific steps for implementing the intervention program outside the treatment setting. There are three things the consultant and consultee can do to facilitate generalization of learning.

1. *Make the intervention plan approximate real life conditions.* For example, if the consultant and teacher wish to get other teachers to implement an academic program for a child, the program *should be* realistic both for the teacher and the child. Otherwise, teachers may not be willing to develop a new instructional program or spend a disproportionate amount of time with the child. Likewise, other teachers may require the child to complete all assignments rather than eighty percent to ninety percent of his/her assignments.

2. *Implement the intervention plan with more than one consultee.* In the classroom the teacher aide or volunteer can implement the plan. Likewise, at home both parents and brothers and sisters may need to be involved to ensure maintainance of the program.

3. *Utilize reinforcers which occur in the client's natural environment.* Money, praise and recognition all occur naturally and should be built into the intervention plan.

Follow-Up

Once the goals and objectives have been attained or when no further interventions are planned, the consultant and consultee should plan a follow-up. Follow-up provides the consultant and consultee an opportunity to check the client's progress and discuss any new problems which may have arisen. Follow-up should occur two to four weeks following the final meeting. However, some provision should be made for the consultee to contact the consultant in the event that serious problems arise which prevent the consultee from implementing the program. When follow-up occurs, the intervention program should be evaluated under the same conditions as it was during the initial phases.

CONSULTING SKILLS INVENTORY

Directions: After each item, check (✓) "yes" or "no" to indicate whether the skill has been demonstrated.

Evaluating Consultation	*Yes*	*No*
1. Determine if outcome objectives have been met.	_____	_____
2. Specify whether criterion levels have been met.	_____	_____
3. Maintain the program.	_____	_____
4. Specify follow-up procedures.	_____	_____

Criterion Test

1. Consultation programs can be evaluated by whether or not
   (a) the consultee wants to continue with the program;
   (b) the client has met the criterion level of performance;
   (c) the baseline level of behavior is decreased;
   (d) the consultee and client are satisfied.

2. Given the following procedures check (✓) those which will maintain the intervention program.

   _____client records own behavior

   _____client's behavior placed under fixed ratio schedule of reinforcement

   _____token reinforcement

   _____transfer program to other consultees

   _____withdraw reinforcement to client

   _____client's behavior placed under intermittent schedule of reinforcement

3. Given the following data and graph in Figure 29, answer the following questions.

	M T W Th F	M T W Th F	M T W Th F
Joe	25 20 20 30 30	45 70 50 75 65	75 85 80 80 80
Harry	20 15 25 15 25	30 25 20 35 30	70 50 75 70 60
	Baseline	Intervention I	Intervention II

	M	T	W	Th	F		M	T	W	Th	F		M	T	W	Th	F
Joe	25	20	20	30	30		45	70	50	75	65		75	85	80	80	80
Harry	20	15	25	15	25		30	25	20	35	30		70	50	75	70	60

| Baseline | Intervention I | Intervention II |

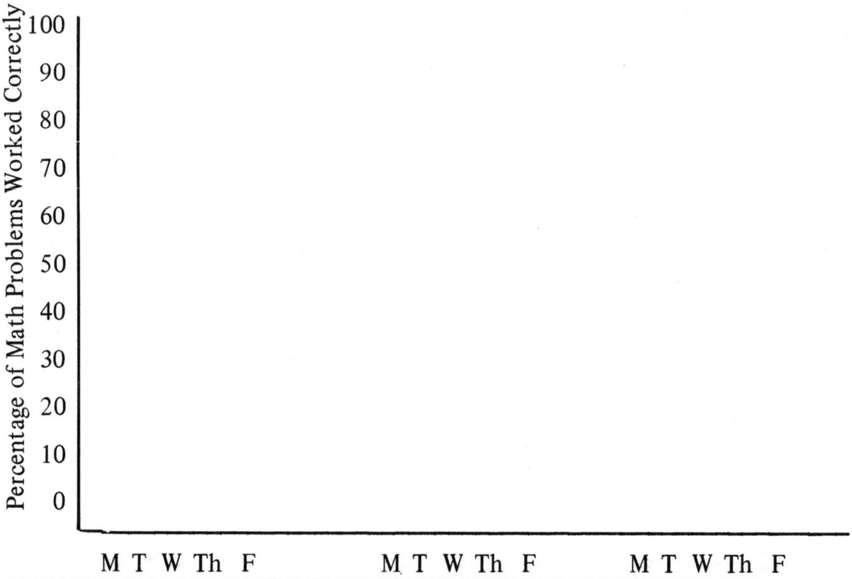

Percentage of Math Problems Worked Correctly

100
90
80
70
60
50
40
30
20
10
0

M T W Th F   M T W Th F   M T W Th F

Figure 33: **Graph To Be Completed**

(a) Label and graph the data on the axes.

(b) What is being measured in this graph?

_____ across _____

(c) For whom is the intervention likely being introduced in the first intervention?

(d) For whom is the treatment likely being introduced in the second intervention?

(e) Describe the change in percent of math problems worked correctly from Baseline to Intervention II.

Joe _____

Harry_____

(f) In 75 words or less, describe the data presented in the graph above.

Criterion Test Answers:

(1) (b)

(2) _____ client records own behavior

     _____ transfer program to other consultees

     _____ client's behavior placed under intermittent schedule of reinforcement.

3. (a)

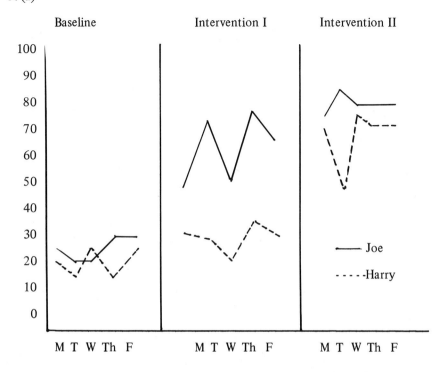

Figure 34: **Completed Graph**

(b)   Percent of correct math problems across Harry and Joe

(c)   Joe

(d)   Harry (Joe continues to receive intervention introduced earlier)

(e)   Joe: more than tripled

Harry: more than tripled

(f)   The percentage of correct math problems was measured for Joe and Harry. At the beginning of the second week, an intervention was introduced with Joe and the percentage of math problems he worked correctly more than doubled from baseline, while little change was observed for Harry. In the third week, the intervention was introduced for Harry. His percentage of math problems worked correctly more than tripled his baseline total; Joe's percent of correct increased slightly during Intervention II.

APPENDIX

CONSULTATION CASE STUDY

After school one day, the fourth grade teacher, Ms. Brown approached the consultant, Mr. Moore, and said, "Shirley Burns' mother would like to talk with you sometime. She's really concerned that Shirley's grades were so poor this grading period and she's having trouble with her at home too. Could you give her a call at home and set up a time for her to see you?"

The consultant followed up on this request and set a time to see Mrs. Burns. The following script is from the first session with Mrs. Burns. (C refers to the consultant, Mr. Moore, and P to the parent, Mrs. Burns.)

		Consultant Techniques
C:	I'm glad you could get off from work, Mrs. Burns.	
P:	Well, I've been wanting to talk with you. Shirley has been very difficult for me to handle for a while but she seems to be getting even worse recently. She's just about too much for me to handle.	*Joining*
C:	Tell me what you mean.	*Asking for clarification*
P:	You know, she just won't mind or do her schoolwork. I just don't know what to do with her.	
C:	Sounds like you're really frustrated and beginning to feel helpless.	*Responding to feelings*
P:	That's for sure. I'm glad for days she has activities after school because she disrupts the whole household when she's home. Then I feel guilty about not wanting her there.	
C:	Your feelings are mixed then. Although you know the house is more pleasant when she's not there, you think you should want her to be there.	
P:	Yes. It doesn't make much sense, does it? How well do you know Shirley?	

C: Not very well. I see her in the classroom occasionally and I've talked with Mrs. Brown about her schoolwork. I've never talked with her alone, though.

P: Do you think you could do that? I think you might get something out of her. She won't tell me why she does the things she does.

C: Well, Mrs. Burns, I might see her once or twice just to get more information about her, but I'd prefer that you and I work together to figure out how to get her to behave better.

Stating role

P: I've really tried everything I know. I can't imagine doing anything else with her.

C: Are you willing to try some different things?

P: Yes, but I can't think what.

C: Well, I'm sure we'll think of some things. But first, I'd like to better understand what she does that you don't like.

Defining the problem

P: OK. I told you she won't mind and she does poorly at school.

C: What do you mean when you say Shirley doesn't mind?

Operationalizing the problem

P: Just that. If I tell her to pick up her clothes, she just doesn't do it. When I tell her to do her homework, she just ignores me.

C: Does she tell you she's not going to do what you tell her or does she just act as though she will and then not follow through?

Determining when the behavior occurs

P: She says things like "OK, later" and then just doesn't do it.

C: When does this usually happen?

P: Mostly right after school when she wants to watch TV.

C: What happens when she doesn't do it?

Determining what maintains the problem

P: Sometimes I get mad and yell at her, but there's not much I can do.

C: So you want Shirley to do what you tell her. And you mentioned her poor schoolwork. Tell me more about that.

Identifying all problem areas

P: Last grading period she got 3 D's and she's always done well in school before. Her teacher says she doesn't turn in her assignments and that she disrupts the class by talking out loud and talking to other students when they're supposed to be working. I've spoken to her about this and told her not to do it, but she denies that she talks to other students.

C: You'd like to see her talk less, then, turn in more assignments, and get better grades.

P: Right! That would certainly make life easier for all of us.

C: We now have - her minding you, completing assignments and improving grades. Are there other things you're concerned about?

P: Yes. Really, I'm bothered that Shirley has so few friends. Well, really, she doesn't have any close friends. And that seems strange to me because Shirley's sister, Marge, who's 10, has friends over all the time. I think Shirley just doesn't know how to act around other kids.

C: How does she act?   *Operationalizing*

P: She's silly.   *the problem*

C: What does she do that's silly?

P: She hits people to get attention or she will interrupt and talk very loudly. She doesn't get invited to parties like Marge does . . . and she doesn't bring anyone home either. It's usually with Marge's friends that she acts so silly. I don't know how she is at school.

C: I could probably have a talk with her teacher sometime to find out.

P: That would help. As I said, I just don't know what to do now.

C: OK, you've mentioned three problem areas -   *Identifying all* Shirley's failure to mind, her poor grades and   *problem areas* her peer relationships. Are there others?

P: No, those about cover everything.

C: Which of these problems is of most immediate   *Prioritizing the* concern to you? Which would you want to   *problems* change first?

P: Getting her to mind. If she did that, it would surely help me.

C: Allright. Let's work on that one first. You've said she minds least right after school when she's watching TV. Is there a particular place where you have the biggest problem?

Determining place where undesirable behavior occurs

P: Yes, usually in the TV room. For one thing, half the time she doesn't seem to hear me. When I tell her to do something, she may not respond at all.

C: You mentioned before that she sometimes says, "OK, later."

Operationalizing the problem behavior

P: Yes, when I raise my voice, she makes a promise to do it later. If I talk in a tone of voice like I'm using with you now, she probably wouldn't even answer.

C: How do you usually react when she doesn't answer?

P: It depends on what I want her to do . . . or what kind of mood I'm in. Sometimes I just go on and do it myself or ask her sister to do it. Other times I yell at her. Then she promises to do it later, and it usually turns into a yelling match, because she doesn't do it at all.

C: Does anyone else have difficulty getting her to mind?

Determining who owns the problem

P: Primarily me. My husband occasionally gets mad at her, but he actually asks her to do very few things. I think she does what she's told at school except for assigned work. Mrs. Brown says she isn't really a discipline problem, but that she just doesn't finish her work.

C: You're the one who is mainly concerned about getting her to mind more then. What have you tried so far to get her to mind?

P: Yelling. Threatening her.

C: How has it worked?

P: It hasn't. That's why I'm here.

C: Well, we'll get our heads together here and come up with *something* that will work, I'll bet. You seem willing to give it another shot.

Getting indication of commitment

P: Oh, sure. I'll do whatever you suggest.

C: Let's work it out together. Now, are you   *Expressing com-*
     satisfied with first working on getting   *mitment to help*
     Shirley to mind and then attacking the other
     concerns?

P: Yes, I'd like to work on that first.

C: OK, we first need some ideas of how often   *Determining*
     Shirley fails to mind, when and where it   *responsibility for*
     happens, and what you do about it. Would   *assessing the*
     you be willing to keep a chart of those things?   *problem*
     It will take some time but we can try to keep
     it simple.

P: Yeah, it might keep me really busy writing all
     that down. Seriously, though I'll do it. Since
     she's gone most of the day, it will only be
     before and after school.

C: Very good. Let's make a chart then that you   *Planning assess-*
     can use. About how many times a day would   *ment procedure*
     you say she doesn't mind?

P: Probably around fifteen. But then some of
     those are when I tell her the second or third
     time to do something.

C: Good point. We'll need that information too.
     OK, we'll need to know what you've told her
     to do, where, when, and what you do when
     she doesn't mind. Can you think of anything
     else we need to include?

P: What about Shirley's response when I tell her
     to do something?

C: Good point! Now, using a chart like this, you
     will have a count of how often she actually
     minds and how often she doesn't. Will this
     be too much to record or would you prefer
     to just take a certain time each day?

P: I think I can write it down every time.

C: Good. Here's the chart then. If you'll do this
     from now until about Friday, that will give us
     about four days of information.

P: Sounds good. You want me to come back
     Friday then?

C: Yes, if you can. How about right after school?

P: Fine. See you about 3:00 P.M. on Friday.

C: OK, just remember, though, that right now you're just getting information on this. We won't be trying anything to change anything until next week.

P: Right. I understand. Thanks.

The following is the consulting session for Friday:

C: Well, how did it go?

P: I got everything written down here. What I found out was that she really does what I tell her to do sometimes and I guess I don't remember those times.

C: Let's take a look at your chart.   *Reviewing information*

Table 12: Assessment Chart

Time		Place	Command	Shirley's Response	Parents Response/What happened after?
Day	Hour				
Mon	3:30	TV room	Do your homework	Nothing	Repeated it louder
Mon	3:32	TV room	Do your homework	"OK. When this program's over"	"OK. Just don't forget"
*Mon	5:30	Kitchen	Set the table.	Did it	Nothing
Mon	6:30	TV room	Help your sister carry those books.	Nothing	Said louder, "Shirley, help your sister carry those books!"
Mon	6:32	TV room	Help your sister carry those books.	"What?"	"Help your sister. Why don't you listen?" (Complained some more) She did it.
Mon	9:00	TV room	It's time to go to bed.	"I don't want to. Let me watch Laverne & Shirley."	"No. Get to bed." She didn't go until 9:20.
*Tues	8:00	Kitchen	Go clean your room and make your bed.	"In a minute." (She did it well.)	Nothing
Tues	3:45	TV room	Shirley will you go to the store for me?	Nothing	Yelled her name. She said "What?"
Tues	3:47	TV room	Shirley will you go to the store for me?	"Why can't Marge go?"	"Because I asked you." She kept sitting and watching TV.
Tues	3:55	TV room	Shirley, I mean it. I need something from the store and Marge is not home.	"You expect me to do everything. Well, this show's about over."	Came to kitchen about 4:00 and went to store.
*Tues	6:00	Kitchen	Help me put the food on the table.	Did it.	

C: You did a good job with this. What do the stars mean here?

P: I added those. Those are the times Shirley did what I asked.

C: Very good. You're right. She did as you asked her several times. Mrs. Burns, did you notice any patterns in the times Shirley did what you wanted or refused to do it?

Noting behavior patterns

P: Well, most of the time she didn't do what I wanted was when she was watching TV. She loves TV and that's about all she does after school. You know, I told you she doesn't have many friends.

C: Right, I remember, and we'll work on that a little later. OK, she often doesn't mind when she's watching TV and the times are usually from right after school until dinner time.

P: Yes, mainly, but then she likes to watch TV after dinner too and she just ignores me then.

C: It seems pretty clear that Shirley doesn't respond much when she's watching TV but that she often does in other situations. Were there any differences in what you did when she minded and when she didn't?

P: Well, when she did I didn't do anything. When she didn't, I sometimes didn't do anything but often I yelled and lectured.

C: Do you think she minds the yelling and lecturing?

P: No, I think she just turns it off.

C: So the consequences of doing what she's told and not doing what she's told are about the same.

P: I guess so. I hadn't really thought of it that way, but I guess it doesn't make much difference to her.

C: Tell me, what would you like Shirley to be doing? What level or degree of minding would be reasonable?

Formulating treatment goals

P: I know she won't always want to do what I tell her but I think she should mind about ninety percent of the time.

C: Let's get this clear. Do you mean ninety percent of the time she should act after being told once?

P: Right. That's what I meant.

C: At any time or place you ask her?

P: Yes.

C: What are some of the roadblocks that get in the way of her minding?

Assessing roadblocks

P: The TV - obviously.

C: Any ideas about how to overcome that roadblock?

Deciding how to overcome road-blocks

P: Maybe not ask her during that time or turn off the TV when I'm asking her something.

C: Both of those ideas sound workable and we need to keep them in mind. They will certainly help overcome the barrier. Now, for what we want to happen - would you just summarize our goal?

Getting consultee to summarize goal

P: To get Shirley to mind ninety percent of the time after being asked only once.

C: OK, good. Now, let's just see how many ideas we can generate to bring this about. What are some things you can think of to get her to mind?

Prompting consultee to generate alternatives

P: Well, as I said before, one thing would be to only ask her to do things when she's not watching TV. Another would be to turn off the TV and ask her.

C: Good. I have two alternatives. Can you think of others?

P: Well, I *could* just stop asking her to do anything. I don't think I like that one though.

C: You don't want that one included then?

P: No. Do you have any ideas?

C: Well, I was thinking another alternative might be to provide good consequences for compliance. For instance, if you praised Shirley when she did what you asked, she might be more likely to comply the next time. Or if TV watching is contingent upon her minding, she would be very motivated to mind.

P: That's true, but I haven't done that because I just felt I'd better leave well enough alone. It's true, though, as you said before that I did about the same thing whether she minded or not. You know, I just thought of something else. Shirley saw the chart I've been keeping just before she left for school this morning and she was very interested. I guess I could make out a chart for her showing when she did and didn't mind.

C: Right. That's another alternative. Still another would be to make out a chart just recording the times she minds and then giving her some kind of reward for this.

P: You mean like money or something?

C: It could be money, but it could be activities or privileges like having someone over for the night. Or getting some time from you or your husband. Or even TV time.

P: Well, she would certainly like that.

C: Any other ideas?

P: No, that's all I can think of.

C: Well, we've got five — only ask her to do something when she's not watching TV, turn off the TV to ask her, praise her when she minds, show her a chart of how often she minds, and keep track of minding and give rewards. Let's talk about the advantages of each of these. How about not asking her to do anything while she's watching TV?

Summarizing alternatives

Prompting consultee to evaluate alternatives

P: She would like that but that would be hard to do. Sometimes, I really need her when she is all wrapped up in TV. Also, that would mean I'd never ask her to do anything right after school or at night.

C: Sounds like you think that alternative needs to be discarded. You don't like it.

P: Right.

C: OK. The second was to turn off the TV and then ask.

P: Really, she would listen that way. But she would probably get mad at me. She really likes TV programs.

C: Do you think the advantages are great
enough to keep this as a possibility?

P: Yes.

C: OK, I'll put a little check by it. What about
praising her when she complies?

P: I probably should do that, but I'm always
afraid it may make her stop.

C: When someone praises you, how do you feel?

P: Oh, real good.

C: And do you feel like doing more or less of
what you were praised for?

P: More. I see what you're saying. Well,
I'll start doing that.

C: You're going to keep this as a possibility
then. What about showing her the chart
of her behavior?

P: She really enjoyed seeing that. She asked
what you were going to do with it. I think
she was kind of embarrassed. She was
surprised, I think, how often she didn't do
what I asked.

C: You think the information may be helpful
to her then?

P: Yes.

C: OK. We'll keep that alternative as a
possibility. And that leaves keeping
a record of compliance and providing
rewards.

P: I'm willing to do that. In fact, I like that
idea.

C: Well, that leaves us with four possibilities: *Prompting*
turn off the TV to ask her to do things, praise *consultee to*
her when she does them, give her information *select the*
(from a chart) about how she's doing, and give *best alternative*
rewards for minding. Which of these or which
combination would you like to try?

P: I think I'd need to turn off the TV to ask her
something and then praise her if she minds.
I could also give her rewards for minding.
Maybe I wouldn't need to show her the chart.

C: Your solution sounds good. Now how are you going to do all this? How will you set it up and when will you start?

Prompting consultee to plan implementation

P: When I get home today, Shirley will ask what we talked about. Should I tell her?

C: I think it would be fine to tell her and to let her know you're interested in getting her to mind better.

P: OK, I'll tell her and I'll also say that I'm going to start turning the TV off when I ask her to do something. Then if she does it, I'll tell her I'm glad or say thanks.

C: How about the rewards?

P: Oh, I guess I'll have to still keep a record of when she minds. Then I'll tell her she can do something good when she minds.

C: Will she know what you're talking about? What does good mean? How will she know she's been good? And how long will she have to be good to get a reward? Also, will the two of you agree that a particular reward is a good one?

P: I see what you mean. Well, how could I do it?

C: I can tell you how some parents handle that. They give one point for each time the child minds. Then they set up a list of activities or whatever and put a point value on them. For instance, it may cost fifteen points to have someone stay all night with you, five points to watch an hour of TV, etc. If Shirley has a list of activities and costs, she can "spend" her points whenever she wants to.

P: That sounds good and I know a lot of things Shirley likes. I can make out a list tonight. Should I ask her if she wants something on it?

C: That would be a good idea. But you have to make sure you don't put anything on the list that you won't let her do. Do you have any questions about giving praise or setting up the reward sheet?

P: No. I think I can do it.

C: How about working on that tonight and giving   *Establishing time*
      me a call tomorrow? We can talk about your   *for follow-up*
      list and how things went with turning off the
      TV and praising Shirley for compliance.

P: OK. I'll call you in the morning.

C: Very good. And good luck on making out
      your list.

The next part of the consultation process is the follow-up session. At this time, the consultant assesses with the consultee whether or not the program is progressing satisfactorily. If there are problems in implementing the program, or if the program is not working, the consultant helps troubleshoot. In this particular case, problems may occur if the reinforcers selected are not powerful or varied enough, if they are not given consistently and on contingency, if Mrs. Burns does not turn off the TV to make a request, etc. Where difficulties exist, the consultant may again go through the problem solving process with the consultee, determining alternative procedures to be implemented.

On the other hand, if the treatment program is working, the consultant should reinforce the consultee's behavior in implementing the program and then begin helping her deal with additional concerns, e.g., completing schoolwork and improving peer relationships. It should be noted, however, that the consultee should continue working with the initial problem behavior until the desired behavior has stabilized. Then, the process described in the typescript would be repeated, substituting a different problem behavior.

BIBLIOGRAPHY

American Psychological Association. *Guidelines for testing minority children.* Washington, D.C., A.P.A., 1964.

Becker, W.C., Engelman, S. & Thomas, D.R. *Teaching 2: Cognitive learning and instruction.* Palo Alto: Science Research Associates, 1975.

Becker, W.C., Engelman, S. & Thomas, D.R. *Teaching: A course in applied psychology.* Chicago: Science Research Associates, 1975.

Benjamin, A. *The helping interview.* 1st ed. Boston: Houghton Mifflin, 1969.

Bergan, J.R. *Behavioral consultation.* Columbus: Charles E. Merrill Publishing Co., 1977.

Bergan, J.R. & Tombari, M.L. The analysis of verbal interactions occurring during consultation. *Journal of School Psychology,* 1975.

Berlin, I.N. Learning mental health consultation history and problems. *Mental Hygiene,* 1964, *48,* 257-266.

Birkimer, J.C. & Brown, J.H. The effects of student self-control on the reduction of children's problem behaviors. *Behavioral Disorders,* 1979, *4,* 131-136.

Borg, W.R., Kelly, M.L., Langer, P. & Gall, M.D. *The minicourse – A microteaching approach to teacher education.* Beverly Hills, California: MacMillan Educational Services, 1970.

Borg, W. Minicourses: Individualized learning packages for teacher education. *Educational Technology,* 1972, *12,* 57-64.

Brokes, A.A. Process model of consultation. In C.A. Parker (Ed.) *Psychological consultation: Helping teachers meet special needs.* Minneapolis: Leadership Training Institute, 1975.

Caplan, G. *The theory and practice of mental health consultation.* New York: Basic Books, 1970.

Carrington, P. The mediator mode of consultation. In D.J. Kurpius and W. Lanning (Eds.) *Psychoeducational consultation: Conference Proceedings.* Bloomington, Ind.: Indiana University, 1976.

Coopersmith, S. *The antecedents of self-esteem.* San Francisco: W.H. Freeman and Company, 1967.

Cossairt, A., Hall, R.V. & Hopkins, B.L. The effects of experimenter's instructions, feedback and praise on teacher praise and student attending behavior. *Journal of Applied Behavior Analysis,* 1973, *6,* 89-100.

Cunningham, R. *Understanding group behavior of boys and girls.* New York: Bureau of Publications, Teachers College, Columbia University, 1951.

211

Davis, L.N. *Planning, conducting, evaluating workshops.* Austin: Learning Concepts, 1974.

Dustin, R. & George, R. *Action counseling for behavior change.* Cranston, R.I.: The Carroll Press, rev. ed., 1977.

Dustin, R. & Burden, C. The counselor as a behavioral consultant. *Elementary School Guidance and Counseling,* 1972, *7,* 14-19.

Edge, D., Brown, C. & Brown, J.H. Counseling students with learning disabilities. In G.R. Walz & L. Benjamin (Eds.), *Counseling exceptional people.* Ann Arbor, MI: ERIC-CAPS, The University of Michigan, 1979.

Gagne, R.M. *The conditions of learning.* 2nd ed. New York: Holt, Rinehart & Winston, 1970.

Gelfand, P.M. & Hartmann, D.P. *Child Behavior: Analysis and Therapy.* Elmsford, N.Y.: Pergamon Press, 1975.

Goldfried, M.R. & Davison, G.C. *Clinical behavior therapy.* New York: Holt, Rinehart & Winston, 1976.

Graziano, A.M. (Ed.). *Behavior therapy with children.* Vol. I. Chicago: Aldine-Atherton, 1971.

Gronlund, N.E. *Preparing crietrion referenced tests for classroom instruction.* New York: MacMillan, 1973.

Houmes, G. Revitalizing inservice training for change. *Educational Technology,* 1974, *19,* 33-39.

Ivey, A.E. *Microcounseling: Innovations in interviewing training.* Springfield, Illinois: Charles C. Thomas, 1972.

Jackson, D.A., Hazel, M.M. & Saudargras, R.A. *A guide to staff training.* Lawrence: University of Kansas Support and Development Center for Follow Through, 1974.

Kimball, R.B. A study of rewards and incentives for teachers. *Phi Delta Kappan,* 1974, *9,* 437.

Kiresuk, T.J. & Sherman, R.E. Goal attainment scaling: A general method for evaluating comprehensive community mental health programs. *Community Mental Health Journal,* 1968, *4,* 443-453.

Kurpius, D.J. & Brubaker, J.C. *Psychoeducational consultation: Definitions – functions – preparation.* Bloomington: Indiana University, 1976.

Kurpius, D.J. & Lanning, W. *Psychological consultation: Conference Proceedings.* Bloomington: Indiana University, 1976.

Mager, R.F. & Pipe, R. *Analyzing performance problems.* Belmont, California: Fearon Publishers, 1970.

Mayer, G.R. Behavioral consulting: Using behavior modification procedures in the consulting relationship. *Elementary School Guidance and Counseling.* 1973, *7,* 114-119.

Moore, R. & Sanner, K. Helping teachers analyze and remedy problems. In J.D. Krumboltz & C.E. Thorensen (Eds.). *Behavioral counseling: Cases and techniques.* New York: Holt, Rinehart & Winston, 1969.

Ojemann, R. *Education in human behavior.* Cleveland: Educational Research Council for America, 1971.

O'Leary, W.D. & O'Leary, S.G. *Classroom management.* New York: Pergamon Press, 1972.

Panyon, M., Boozer, H. & Morris, N. Feedback to attendants as a reinforcer for applying operant techniques. *Journal of Applied Behavior Analysis,* 1970, *3,* 1-4.

Parker, C.A. (Ed.). *Psychological consultation: Helping teachers meet special needs.* Minneapolis: Leadership Training Institute, 1975.

Piers, E.V. & Harris, D.B. Age and other correlates of self-concept in children. *Journal of Educational Psychology,* 1964, *55,* 91-95.

Popham, W.J. An approaching peril: Criterion-referenced tests. *Phi Delta Kappan,* 1974, *55,* 614-615.

Schmidt, J.A. Research techniques for counselors: The multiple baseline. *Personnel and Guidance Journal,* 1974, *53,* 200-206.

Stewart, N.R., Winborn, B.B., Johnson, R.G., Burks, H.M. & Engelkes, J.R. *Systematic counseling.* Englewood Cliffs, N.J.: Prentice Hall Publishing Co., 1978.

Stumphauzer, J.S. A low-cost "bug-in-the-ear" sound system for modification of therapist, parent and patient behavior. *Behavior Therapy,* 1971, *2,* 249-250.

Sulzer-Azaroff, B. & Mayer, G.R. *Applying behavior analysis procedures with children and youth.* New York: Holt, Rinehart & Winston, 1977.

Sundel, M. and Sundel, S.S. *Behavior modification in the human services: A systematic introduction to concepts and applications.* New York: John Wiley, 1975.

Tharp, R.G. The triadic model of consultation: Current considerations. In C.A. Parker (Ed.). *Psychological consultation: Helping teachers meet special needs.* Minneapolis: Leadership Training Institute, 1975.

Tharp, R.G. & Wetzel, R.J. *Behavior modification in the natural environment.* New York: Academic Press, 1969.

Vriend, J. & Dyer, W.W. Vital components in conducting the initial counseling interview. *Educational Technology,* 1974, *14,* 24-32.

Wahler, R.G. & Cormier, W.H. The ecological interview: A first step in outpatient child behavior therapy. *Journal of Behavior Therapy and Experimental Psychiatry,* 1970, *1,* 279-289.

Wetzel, R.J. & Patterson, J.R. Technical developments in classroom behavior analysis. In B.C. Etzel, J.M. LeBlanc & D.M. Baur (Eds.). *New developments in behavioral research: Theory, methods and applications.* In honor of Sidney W. Bijou. Hinsdale, N.J.: Lawrence Erlbaum Associates, 1975.

Whitley, A.D. & Sulzer, B. Reducing distruptive behavior through consultation. *Personnel and Guidance Journal,* 1970, *48,* 836-841.

INDEX